YOUR PERSONALITY AND THE SPIRITUAL LIFE

D1146434

Your Personality and the Spiritual Life

REGINALD JOHNSON

MONARCH
Crowborough

First published 1988 by Victor Books USA as *Celebrate, my soul*
Published 1995 under this title by Victor Books, USA
First British edition 1995

British Library Cataloguing Data
A catalogue record for this book is available
from the British Library

ISBN 1 85424 340 3

Designed and produced by Bookprint Creative Services
P.O. Box 827, BN21 3YJ, England for
MONARCH PUBLICATIONS
Broadway House, The Broadway,
Crowborough, E. Sussex TN6
Text reproduced from the original setting
by arrangement with Victor Books, a
division of Scripture Press Publications Inc.
Printed in Great Britain

To my parents
Hazel and Clarence
who loved me
into discovering my Creation Gifts

and to my wife
and best friend
Jo
who has encouraged
and enriched my life

and to our children
Wesley, Joshua, Katie, and Nathan
who are a constant source
of wonder and joy

CONTENTS

Preface

Would you like to understand yourself better? Would you like to discover the special gifts with which God has endowed you from birth? Would you like to see how these gifts affect your relationships and to understand how your personality colors your spiritual life? Would you like to find out why some devotional disciplines and patterns may be more helpful to you than others? Would you like to know how your temperament can be enriched? Would you like to discover how God might be able to use your special traits in His kingdom purposes?

God never intended that your personality be a handicap but an endowment. He has entrusted you with your own special talents and characteristics. When you are able to recognize these gifts and offer them back to Him to cultivate and expand them, you will discover new dimensions of discipleship.

We always find our true identity in relationship with Jesus Christ. After all, He is the One who can help us discover our true selves and fill these selves with life and love.

I invite you to join me on a journey through these pages. We will explore these things together and will come to realize more fully than ever what James meant when he wrote, "Every perfect gift and every good endowment is from above, and comes down from the Father of lights with whom there is no variation or shadow of turning" (James 1:17).

Reginald Johnson
Asbury Theological Seminary
Wilmore, Kentucky
1995

Chapter One

The Soulprint

As I have led retreats on personality and the spiritual life, the one question I have been asked more than any other is this, "Does God ever change a person's personality?" Phrased this way, the question sounds too academic and theoretical. But I suspect that underneath, there is often a burning personal issue. I recognize it because it has bubbled up from within me as well. "Can God really change *me?*" This is a question often asked by those recently converted to Christ. For all the vitality of their new relationship to God through Christ, they have come to feel that not everything got converted. They were assured, "Therefore, if anyone is in Christ, he is a new creation; old things have passed away; behold, all things have become new" (2 Corinthians 5:17). Did they misunderstand the promise?

Doug has a sharp mind. Quick and perceptive, he's the sort of person who can take a problem apart and lay out its various components, then put them back together with remarkable rapidity. He is an analyst—in every department of life. Speaking to me about his spiritual life, he said, "When I hear people talk about their feelings of love or faith, it is as if I were standing on the outside looking in. I wish I had that capacity—to really *feel* things, I mean. If being a Christian is defined by having that kind of inner emotion, I guess I have a long way to go. I'm wired rationally. Those who first introduced me to the faith talked as if I needed to park my head at the door—or leave it at the altar. I was told that I would receive a new heart. I kept waiting for a personality makeover, but it never happened."

Jane, on the other hand, is a sensitive person. Her compassionate heart enables her to empathize with the hurts of another, but it sometimes creates problems for her, particularly when she is oversensitive. If someone makes a comment that hurts her feelings, she may back off from that person, and perhaps from other people too. She carries the hurt inside so that it casts a cloud on all she does. Alienated from others and unhappy with herself, she is at times so crippled by a feeling of guilt that she thinks she is unfit spiritually. When going through such a patch, she tends to be preoccupied with herself and lacks the confidence to step forward with her gifts in service to others. Too often she finds herself praying, "O God, I just wish You would change me so I wouldn't have to live like this!"

"Be all that you can be!" was an effective advertising slogan simply because it hooked into a basic heart-desire. We really do want to be *all* that we can be. You probably share my conviction that in Christ we can fulfill our God-given potential. But perhaps you are also wondering about the process. *How does God interact with us to bring about changes in the habits of our hearts and the patterns by which we relate to others and ourselves?* This will be the guiding question for the pages ahead.

Self-fulfillment?

Before we move too far, we need a foundation upon which to build. We hear a lot of talk these days about self-fulfillment. Apart from life in relationship to God, self-fulfillment lacks dimension, direction, and dynamic. When we do not see our lives against the backdrop of the eternal God and the larger context of meaning which He gives, our existence is constricted and centered basically upon ourselves. Such a narrow focus ends up corrupting life rather than enhancing it.

Christianity has a much greater concern than what is usually contained in the term self-fulfillment. In his letter to the Ephesians, Paul establishes a basis for our self-understanding. In the opening verses of the first chapter, he assures us that God had us in mind before the world was founded. He designed us to live as His own children. He arranged for our adoption through Jesus Christ. In Christ, at the cost of His own blood, we have been redeemed. He has given us insight into the secret of His plan for the universe. When we put our confidence in Him we are stamped, as it were, with His Spirit. This enables us to live out our destiny, the very purpose of our existence—to be holy (wholly His) and blameless before Him, and, therefore, be a credit to Him in all that we are and do. We are to "grow up in Him" (in Christ) in every way, and to "arrive at that real maturity—that measure of development which is meant by 'the fullness of Christ' " (Ephesians 4:13, PH). When you and I look at ourselves in this way, we are dealing with something greater than self-fulfillment. It has to do with Christfulness.

Be all that you can be? Absolutely! But don't set your sights so low that you define your possibilities by merely natural standards. The starting point is this: You cannot begin to understand your full potential outside of a relationship with God, who has endowed you with all of your traits and abilities.

When you look at things from this vantage point, you begin to see that the real issue is not your personality concerns at all. More significant by far is this vast, loving God whom you dare to call "Father"! When He becomes more important than anything else to you, things begin to click into proper perspective. There must be a self-giving to Him before there can be any true self-realization in you. As C.S. Lewis said:

> Christ will indeed give you a real personality, but you must not go to Him for the sake of that. As long as your own personality is what you are bothering about, you are not going to Him at all. The very first step is to try to forget about the self altogether. Your real, new self (which is Christ's and also yours, and yours just because it is His) will not come as long as you are looking for it. It will come as you are looking for Him.[1]

In order to understand the meaning of this real, new self in Jesus Christ, we will begin by focusing upon the Lord Himself. His personality corresponded to His teaching. He was what He preached. His personality was the instrument through which God's good news was communicated to our kind. Let's look at some of His essential qualities and traits as they emerge from the Gospel portraits of Jesus. This will help us understand the way in which God may want to move us toward maturity.

In our approach to Jesus' personality, we will draw from a widely accepted theory of Carl Jung which was further developed and applied by Isabel Briggs Myers, especially in her book, *Gifts Differing*. There she presents the four scales upon which our main differences from one another can be registered.[2]

✠ In our orientation toward life, are we mostly inward turning (introvertive) or outward turning (extrovertive)?

✠ Do we prefer to gather information by way of our five senses (sensing) or through our inner sixth sense (intuition)?

✠ Is our decision-making more likely to flow from critical analysis (thinking) or from value assessments (feeling)?

✠ Do we enjoy an ordered lifestyle, where we live by schedule and plan (judging)? Or do we prefer an open lifestyle, where we approach life with a spirit of flexibility and spontaneity (perceptive)?

When we apply these questions to Jesus' life, we find a striking balance. His life was marked by the capacity to move freely between the two poles in each dimension, responding appropriately and wisely as the situation demanded.

Extroversion and Introversion

Jesus was dedicated to practical service and down-to-earth ministry to others. Every page of the Gospels shimmers in the light of His self-giving life. Whether He was preaching, teaching, healing, or counseling, virtue flowed from Him. His energy was focused outward toward others, the mark of a true extrovert!

However, He recognized that He could not continue giving nonstop. Even though God's love moved powerfully through Him, bringing healing and hope to those whose lives He touched, and even though a stream of needy persons seemed to flow endlessly in His direction, He did not continue in constant motion. He recognized His own limitations as well as the rhythms of life which the Creator had established. So His active life was balanced by withdrawal for reflection and prayer. He would create spaces of solitude in the late hours of the night or in the predawn darkness. He might find places for seclusion on a lonely hilltop, in a grove of olive trees, or in some patch of desert wilderness. However great were the needs of people, and however much God was working through His ministry, He knew that He could not live in perpetual motion—always giving out to others and never taking in for Himself.

His energy radiated outward in ministry, but He also allowed energy to flow into His life, renewing Him in times of solitude and retreat. His outer, active life moved Him toward the inner life of reflection and prayer. Just as the force of the water smooths pebbles in a stream, so His mind washed over experiences, forming and polishing them into insights and understandings about the very principles underlying life. And when He emerged to speak again, these thoughts were communicated with the authority which comes only from the uniting of simplicity and authentic experience. Even as action had moved Him into reflection, solitude prepared Him again for encounter. His extrovertive life was balanced by His introvertive life.

Sensing and Intuition

Jesus was vitally alive in all His senses. He was tuned in to the world around Him. His observations of nature gave color to His teaching and enabled Him to communicate His ideas. No one can easily forget His descriptions of the sower and the seed, the vine and the gardener, the wheat and the weeds. He was equally observant of people. He never seemed so preoccupied with His own thoughts (and there were plenty of occasions when He had every right to have been!) that He missed the verbal and nonverbal communications of others. In the push and shove of the crowd, He was aware of the touch of a woman longing for healing. Even as the shadows of Calvary were falling across the road to Jerusalem, He noticed a little man watching Him from his perch up in a sycamore tree. With all the pressure of apparently unfinished business, He could still take time to welcome warmly a young child at His knee. Jesus was alive in all His senses and seemed aware of everything around Him.

But Jesus was aware of another kind of data as well—that which comes from what we call the sixth sense or intuition. "Before Philip called you," He said to an astonished Nathanael, "when you were under the fig tree, I saw you" (John 1:48). And He responded to the Samaritan woman's comment about not having a husband, "You have well said, 'I have no husband,' for you have had five husbands, and the one whom you now have is not your husband" (4:17-18). After granting a man forgiveness of his sins (which He intuited as the cause of his paralysis), He "perceived in His spirit" that some of the scribes were thinking He had blasphemed because He had dared to forgive sins. "Why do you reason thus in your hearts?" He challenged them.

Does this mean that Jesus experienced *all* of our limitations? Does it mean that He could know only what ordinary people were capable of knowing? Does it mean that He could not have special revelations and insights which could only be explained by His divine nature and unique relationship to God? Theologians have wrestled with these questions through the centuries. Some have answered with an emphatic "Yes!" while others have been just as adamant with a resounding "No!"

Personally, I have no difficulty with the thought that Jesus could receive special knowledge from God. After all, the experience of the Transfiguration, which three disciples were privileged to witness, included a conversation between Jesus and those special visitors to which they were not privy. However, the truth of the Incarnation must imply, among other things, that Jesus had the same kind of nervous system, brain structure, and mental functions as we do—including intuition. It is my opinion that some of the experiences recorded in the Gospels might show the extraordinary development of this natural capacity, rather than superhuman abilities. Seen this way, the incarnation of the Son of God not only reveals the true character of God in terms that we can see, but also displays the full potential of a human life which has been unified by God through love.

While being observant of life, Jesus knew that things were more than they seemed. He discerned inner meanings, discovered underlying and eternal principles, and could vividly picture the unseen realm, even while relating to the visible one. In Jesus' life, sensing and intuition were both given their rightful place, providing Him with the fullest possible range of information as He sought to do the Heavenly Father's will.

Thinking and Feeling

It is not difficult to see Jesus' effectiveness with the tools of thought—logic, analytical skill, reasoning ability. On so many pages of the Gospels, we see Jesus' confrontations with His opposition. Whenever He perceived that the issue was one of Truth versus Error, He met it head-on. Whenever there was evidence that religious leaders were teaching things which would only increase people's burdens or further remove them from the good news of the Father's love, Jesus moved in with incisive logic and clearly reasoned rebuttals. Regardless of how emotionally charged the atmosphere, His thought was always direct and clear, and liberating to those who believed.

But we also see in Jesus another way of handling situations. There were occasions when He laid aside the impersonal reasoning approach in preference for a response based on deeply felt values, empathy, and compassion. Those were the times He chose to respond from the heart and not just the head. "Suffer the little children to come unto Me and forbid them not" was spoken at a time when logic would have dictated that He had more important matters which needed His attention. "Neither do I condemn thee," He said to the woman who had been caught in the act of adultery. "Go and sin no more." This was spoken on an occasion when purely legal reasoning left only one conclusion—guilt, punishable by stoning.

The contrast is important. When dealing with legal disputes, theoretical debates, or attempts to undermine people's faith, Jesus used the thinking approach. In such situations, it was critical to evaluate arguments, marshal evidence, and clarify the issues. Truth was at stake. However, when Jesus was dealing with seeking, broken, wayward people, although He might begin with the head (as He dealt with their questions or misunderstandings), He moved instinctively to the heart. He looked at their lives and situations and demonstrated by word and deed how God felt about them. Life was at stake. These latter encounters were marked by warmth of compassion and depth of understanding. Such gifts were appropriate in an arena where personal need or spiritual hunger predominated.

So in His being, Jesus wedded thinking and feeling, the cognitive and the affective, allowing each its full expression according to the appropriateness of the occasion.

Judging and Perception

It is sometimes difficult for Christians to keep in mind that Jesus was a practicing Jew. The statement "He went to the synagogue as was His custom" is a basic clue to the structure of His life. His years, His weeks, and His days were lived by Judaism's rhythm of ritual and festival, custom and tradition. He understood the rituals' meaning and the festivals' significance, but He would not allow these customs to become impersonal. He would not separate outer forms from their inner substance. These things were never allowed to become ends in themselves, but were always used as means of remembering and glorifying God. Jesus lived an ordered life.

But look at Him again and you will see the other side as well. There were occasions when system and order had to give way and precedence be given to persons and their needs. The planned itinerary had to make room for the unexpected encounter. Sometimes the very forms needed to be changed in the light of new realities — old wineskins replaced by new ones in order to contain the fresh wine of the new kingdom. Jesus lived an open and spontaneous life.

The balance of opposites here, as in the case of the other polarities, was not a bland mean between two extremes. It was not a simple mathematical average. Rather, He demonstrated His capacity for a wise and appropriate response, the ability to do as the occasion required, as He lived out of the center where His life was grounded in God. Jesus lived a balanced life.

Maturing Spiritually: Living a Christful Life

It is important for us to see Jesus' personal qualities for two reasons. On the one hand, it enables us to celebrate whatever positive traits are ours, even though we possess them in a lesser measure than we see in Jesus. It helps us realize how aspects of personality can become channels for conveying the grace of God. The other reason we begin with a focus on Jesus is that it helps us to appreciate why we need the body of Christ so desperately. Since none of us possesses all the qualities of personality in perfect symmetry, we need each other for balance and wholeness. Others not only contribute their strengths and shore up the places where we are weak, but they also can be used of God to stretch and develop us more fully. In these ways God is moving us toward greater maturity in Christ—toward Christfulness. You may have picked up this book in order to find out *how* this happens. How can we cooperate more fully for growth into Christfulness, which is God's goal for us?

One of the great spiritual classics, perhaps the favorite of the German reformer, Martin Luther, is the little book *Theologica Germanica*. The slim volume is packed with spiritual insight. Here is a quote worth pondering.

> It may be commendable to ask, hear about, and gather information concerning good and holy persons, what they have done and suffered, or how they have lived and how God has worked and willed in and through them.
>
> But it is a hundredfold better that man deeply within himself learns and understands the what and the how of his life, what God is working and doing in him, and how God wishes to use him and not to use him.[3]

Soulprinting: Discovering Your Personality Type

When I was eight years old, our family made a pilgrimage to Washington, D.C. One of the highlights of that visit was our tour of the FBI building. I remember the display which explained the fingerprinting method of identification. Just imagine, no two prints are alike! Each person has a unique configuration of tiny lines and grooves on each finger. But how could the staff of the FBI ever find that one particular match, even if a clear print had been lifted at the site of a crime? It was explained that although we are all different, all fingerprints fall into four main types (loops, arches, whorls, and composites). These main types are further separated into subtypes. They are classified and divided according to type, pattern, and ridges. So, without reference to name, two prints can be matched in minutes!

Through the work of Carl Jung in Europe and Isabel Briggs Myers in this country, a similar work of classification has been done in the area of personality. Their work has made it possible for us to observe and identify some of our own characteristics.

By discovering our own soulprint or personality type, we can appreciate our God-given attributes, identify some of our special areas of vulnerability and weakness, and discover the kinds of resources which might be most conducive for nurturing our relationship with Christ. In the next chapter you will learn how to identify the basic types of personality.

Before you go any further, however, take a few minutes to do the following "Personality Type Concepts Exercise." It will help you begin to think about some of the things which have contributed to the forming of your own unique soul.

Personality Type
Concepts Exercise

Explanation

This exercise is designed to help you understand the meaning of the four preference "scales" of the Myers-Briggs Personality Type Theory. It will enable you to begin to think about the application of that theory to your own life. *This is only an exercise*, not a scientifically designed instrument. If this theory has proven helpful I recommend that you take the Myers-Briggs Type Indicator from someone in your locality who is qualified to administer it (usually a counselor or an educator).

Instructions

This Personality Type Exercise is divided into four sections.
   A. Orientation
   B. Perception
   C. Decision-making
   D. Lifestyle

1. Each number contains two questions which relate to opposite kinds of behaviors or traits. Using the scale underneath each set of descriptions, circle the number which best indicates your preferred ways of living. You *may* circle a number under each statement if you believe that both descriptions would apply to you. Example:

Are you easily bored when you are alone? | Or, do you enjoy solitude in order to spend time in your own thoughts?

E-5   (4)   3   2   1   0   (1)   2   3   4   5-I

2. The numbers on the scale below each set of questions are your shorthand answers and have the following meanings:

> 5 - Always true for me
> 4 - True most of the time
> 3 - True about half of the time
> 2 - Sometimes true
> 1 - Only occasionally true

So, in the example in #1 above, the E-4 indicates that you have a fairly strong preference in that direction, while your I-1 shows that you have only a slight tendency in the opposite direction.

3. Always go with your initial response.

4. Try to respond in terms of how you *prefer* to live, not how you think you should live. Try to express your own preference and not mirror what you think others expect of you, or even what your home or job situation demands from you.

5. Scoring instructions are given at the end of this exercise. Read them after you have completed the following seven pages.

Orientation

1. Do you find that your attention flows naturally to the people and things around you?

   Or, do you find that, whenever possible, you prefer to occupy yourself with your own inner world of thoughts and ideas?

   E-5   4   3   2   1 | 1   2   3   4   5-I

2. Would you characterize yourself as outgoing?

   Or, would you describe yourself as basically a reserved person?

   E-5   4   3   2   1 | 1   2   3   4   5-I

3. Is your energy renewed by being with others?

   Or, even though you enjoy others' presence, do you find that you need solitude to recharge your batteries?

   E-5   4   3   2   1 | 1   2   3   4   5-I

4. Are you rather easy to get to know?

   Or, are you reluctant to allow others into your private world?

   E-5   4   3   2   1 | 1   2   3   4   5-I

5. Do you find it easy to think out loud?

   Or, do you feel that you need to turn inward in order to collect and organize your thoughts before you speak?

   E-5   4   3   2   1 | 1   2   3   4   5-I

6. Are you rather expressive of your feelings?

   Or, do you mostly keep your feelings to yourself?

   E-5   4   3   2   1 | 1   2   3   4   5-I

7. When you are under stress, do you seek the company of others in order to sort things out?

Or, when under stress, do you require a measure of seclusion so that you can pull things together?

E-5　　4　　3　　2　　1　　◉　　1　　2　　3　　4　　5-I

8. Do you tend to act first and then think later?

Or, do you tend to reflect and reflect and (perhaps) eventually get around to action?

E-5　　4　　3　　2　　1　　◉　　1　　2　　3　　4　　5-I

Perception

1. Do you depend on your five senses in order to gather data about what's happening?

Or, do you rely more on your intuitions and hunches in order to form impressions about what's going on?

S-5　　4　　3　　2　　1　　◉　　1　　2　　3　　4　　5-N

2. Do you prefer straightforward ways of speaking and writing—the more specific and concrete the better?

Or, do you like a speaker or writer to use images and symbols which allow you to engage your own imagination?

S-5　　4　　3　　2　　1　　◉　　1　　2　　3　　4　　5-N

3. Are you an observer of tradition, one who does not easily break with custom?

Or, are you able to break with tradition whenever it seems restrictive and to lay aside customs which seem too cumbersome for a new situation?

S-5　　4　　3　　2　　1　　◉　　1　　2　　3　　4　　5-N

4. Does the here and now keep your attention?

Or, are you fascinated by what could be, and find that those possibilities occupy your thoughts?

S-5   4   3   2   1   0   1   2   3   4   5-N

5. Do you have trouble seeing the forest for the trees?

Or, are you a person who often cannot see the trees for the forest?

S-5   4   3   2   1   0   1   2   3   4   5-N

6. Are you a practical sort of person with a common sense approach to things?

Or, are you an ingenious and inventive sort of person with a creative approach to things?

S-5   4   3   2   1   0   1   2   3   4   5-N

7. If someone hangs a new picture or puts a new plant on the table, will you almost always notice it?

Or, are you often rather unobservant of your surroundings?

S-5   4   3   2   1   0   1   2   3   4   5-N

8. Are you a steady, dependable kind of person who can be counted on for the long haul?

Or, do you tend to work by inspiration and find that when your vision for a task fades, so does your energy?

S-5   4   3   2   1   0   1   2   3   4   5-N

Decision-making

1. Are you generally secure in basing your decisions on an objective analysis weighing the pros and cons of a situation?

   Or, regardless of the pros and cons score, are you more secure when you feel that your decision is being based on values which are important to you and to others?

   T-5   4   3   2   1   0   1   2   3   4   5-F

2. Can you usually get on with your job, regardless of relational harmony?

   Or, do you find that harmonious relationships are essential for you to function effectively in a situation?

   T-5   4   3   2   1   0   1   2   3   4   5-F

3. Does making a critical evaluation come more naturally for you than speaking an appreciative word?

   Or, are you more spontaneous with an appreciative word than with a critical evaluation?

   T-5   4   3   2   1   0   1   2   3   4   5-F

4. When forced to choose, do you place truthfulness above tactfulness?

   Or, when you face a crunch, do you place tactfulness above truthfulness?

   T-5   4   3   2   1   0   1   2   3   4   5-F

5. Do you find that your contribution to a group often lies in your ability to help people see objectively?

   Or, do you find your contribution to others usually flows from your ability to empathize and to help people stay mindful of other's feelings?

   T-5   4   3   2   1   0   1   2   3   4   5-F

6. In conversation, are you more concise than expressive?

Or, in conversations, are you more expressive than concise?

T-5   4   3   2   1   0   1   2   3   4   5-F

7. Do you believe that people are more apt to make the wrong move if they go with their heart rather than their head?

Or, do you believe that people are more likely to make the wrong move if they go with their head rather than their heart?

T-5   4   3   2   1   0   1   2   3   4   5-F

8. Are you more impersonal, with more interest in things than in people?

Or, are you more personal, with more interest in people than in things?

T-5   4   3   2   1   0   1   2   3   4   5-F

Lifestyle

1. Do you prefer to plan your work and work your plan?

Or, do you like to leave your schedule open so that you can respond to changing events?

J-5   4   3   2   1   0   1   2   3   4   5-P

2. Do your basic contributions to a group often stem from being systematic, orderly, planned, and decisive?

Or, are the attributes which you bring to a group such things as spontaneity, open-mindedness, tolerance, and adaptability?

J-5   4   3   2   1   0   1   2   3   4   5-P

3. Do you enjoy bringing things to completion—finishing the task?

Or, do you like the feeling of getting new things started and having many things going at the same time?

J-5   4   3   2   1   0   1   2   3   4   5-P

4. Do you like to get the information you need and bring things to a decisive conclusion?

Or, is it hard for you to come to closure because you are unsure when you've ever gathered sufficient information?

J-5   4   3   2   1   0   1   2   3   4   5-P

5. Are you the sort of person who likes having standard operating procedures and set routines for doing things?

Or, do you prefer trying out new and fresh ways of doing recurring tasks so that you won't get into a rut?

J-5   4   3   2   1   0   1   2   3   4   5-P

6. Would the phrase "A place for everything and everything in its place" be descriptive of your lifestyle?

Or, are you more scattered and disorganized in your ways?

J-5   4   3   2   1   0   1   2   3   4   5-P

7. Is it unsettling for you to have matters up in the air and undecided?

Or, do you prefer keeping your options open for as long as possible, so you won't miss something?

J-5   4   3   2   1   0   1   2   3   4   5-P

8. Is it a greater weak- | Or, do you think that it may
   ness for a person to be | be a greater weakness when
   too laid-back than for | one is too task-oriented than
   the person to be too | for the person to be too laid-
   task-oriented? | back?

J-5   4   3   2   1 | 1   2   3   4   5-**P**

Scoring the Exercise

1. Score each section of the exercise separately.
2. Add the numbers circled in each column.
3. Place your totals in the appropriate spaces below.

    A. Orientation   E ____   I ____
    B. Perception   S ____   N ____
    C. Decision-making   T ____   F ____
    D. Lifestyle   J ____   P ____

4. Go back to #3 above and circle the letter in each set which has the highest score. The circled cluster of letters suggests your type. The example below can guide you.

      E 15   I (30)

      S 19   N (28)

     T (35)   F 20

      J 10   P (30)

In this example, the person's personality type may be INTP.

5. Whenever your scores in a given set are as much as 10 points (or more) apart, your preference is clearer. Less than a 10-point difference means that a strong inclination in one direction contrasted to the other is not indicated by this exercise. In the example above, the person had only a 9-point difference between S and N. Although S is circled, the

individual will need to do some further reflection to determine the accuracy of this exercise.

6. This exercise simply introduces you to the meaning of the four preference scales and it is not a scientifically designed instrument. Hopefully it has enabled you to consider the application of this for your life and has stirred sufficient interest for you to take the Myers-Briggs Type Indicator yourself.

7. As you read this book, test the insight you've obtained from the exercise with the appropriate chapter. If it doesn't seem to fit, find the chapter which seems to describe you best.

Chapter Two

The Creation Gifts

Sometimes help comes from unexpected sources. Some years ago I found myself in the midst of what John Bunyan would have called the Slough of Despond. I don't remember what had led to that season of discouragement and self-pity. Perhaps someone had disappointed me. Perhaps I had come up against criticism, or some dream had smashed into the wall of concrete reality.

Maybe I was not measuring up to my own idealistic standards or was feeling inadequate in comparison to what I thought were another's superior gifts or abilities. Whatever the cause, I had hit a low point. It was during that experience that a colleague handed me the Myers-Briggs Type Indicator, with which he was experimenting for possible use as a teaching aid. I am typically skeptical of such things, but decided to give it a try.

When the inventory had been scored and I read my profile, I experienced a sense of instant self-recognition. Lights came on as I began to sort through my recent experiences, realizing the interconnections between my personality and some of my struggles. My wife filled out the indicator too. In subsequent days she and I shared a lot of laughter, as our new discoveries about ourselves helped us get a handle on some of our frustrations with each other! My new insights also became helpful for understanding some of my own spiritual needs; they began to prove helpful in my ministry as well.

The Four Preferences

At the end of the last chapter you were asked to do the Personality Type Concepts Exercise in order to gain some familiarity with the Myers-Briggs Type theory. Now you are ready to start looking at some of its applications in your own life. We will start with the four letters which resulted from your experiment with that exercise.

In chapter 1, in our observations about the balance in Jesus' life, we utilized the idea of the four sets of preferences which life presents to each of us.

✠ *Orientation.* Is your life mostly oriented to things going on outside yourself (Extroversion—E) or does your attention gravitate more naturally to your own thoughts and musings whenever possible (Introversion—I)?

✠ *Perception.* Do you rely on and develop more fully your capacity to use your five senses (Sensing—S) or do you prefer to tap into your inner sixth sense (Intuition—N) for information about life?

✠ *Decision-making.* Do you put more stock in logical analysis and objective, impersonal, rational thought (Thinking—T) in your decision-making process? Or do you ultimately put more weight upon your subjective evaluation of the situation (Feeling—F)?

✠ *Lifestyle.* Do you enjoy approaching life from an ordered and structured standpoint (Judging—J) or in an open, spontaneous manner (Perception—P)?

The items under each of the headings in the Personality Type Concepts Exercise provided you with examples of some of the characteristics which are common for the four scales.

Although each of us use all eight options in the course of everyday life, we usually prefer one function over the other in each set. As a result we tend to rely on that side of our personality and may be better at it as well. Of course, we may sometimes find ourselves in situations which push us to exercise our weaker side more than we would ordinarily choose. If you are currently in such a situation, you may discover that it even influences the way you respond to the questions.

The point is that your personality is shaped by your preferences and those preferences are still within you, even if they are sometimes covered over by the demands of your life. It is the dynamic interaction of your set of preferences which produces what we call personality type.

**The Weight of Preference
Produces Personality Type**

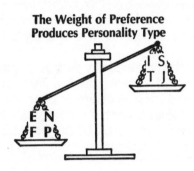

Your Beginning Gift

Whether you are a more introvertive or extrovertive person, you have one mental function (either thinking, feeling, intuiting or sensing) which is your favorite process. It is the element which, more than any other, shapes the contours of your soul. It is a kind of fundamental endowment, representing your special giftedness.

The Plains Indians had as their organizing philosophy of life the "Medicine Wheel." The concept was a rich one. A circle might be drawn on the earth with a stone at each of the four points of the compass. Each of the "directions" was depicted by a special color and a "medicine animal." Each direction stood for one of the four "beginning gifts" with which each person was endowed by the Creator. For example, gold or yellow stood for the East and the eagle was the medicine animal. Since the eagle could fly high and see far, it was used to represent the beginning gift of "seeing" or "observation" (sensing). The bear was selected for the power of the West. The Native Americans noted how it hibernated for long periods of time, so they used it to represent the beginning gift of "inseeing" or "insight" (intuition). Black was the color for the West in their artwork. The North was symbolized by the buffalo and stood for the beginning gift of wisdom (thinking). Since the North is where the snows seemed to originate, white was the symbolic color for the North. Finally, the South was represented by the field mouse. Since this little creature seemed to bump and feel its way through the tall prairie grass, it was said to stand for the power of touch (feeling). Green was the decorative color for the South since it was the direction from which the warm weather seemed to arrive, bringing in the season of growth.

The Plains Indians believed that each person was born with such a beginning gift—thinking, feeling, intuition, or observation. So, on their shields, decorative belts, or other places, the individual would depict his or her special gift by the use of the appropriate symbols and color. They understood that each person was born with this particular strength, a gift from the Creator.

What would you say is your own beginning gift? A clue might have been given as you worked through the Personality Type Exercise. Although it is not a scientific instrument with the sophistication of the Myers-Briggs Type Indicator, perhaps it will give you a useful place from which to begin thinking about yourself.

Giftedness

The giftedness with which I am dealing is what I like to call God's creation gift (contrasted to God's re-creation gifts of the Spirit). Your personality is a creation gift from God. James reminds us that "every good endowment and every complete gift must come from above, from the Father of all lights, with whom there is never the slightest . . . shadow of inconsistency" (James 1:17, PH). I appreciate Thomas Merton's expression that our personality types are talents given to us by the Lord, with which we are to trade until Jesus comes.[1]

When we have entered into a new, personal relationship with God through Jesus Christ, our creation gift is redeemed by Him. We offer it back to Him for His glory, so that we can fulfill His purposes in our lives. Of course, God also gives us spiritual gifts to enable our ministry to Him, but even these spiritual gifts are expressed through our personalities which have been redeemed and are being converted to Him.

This does not imply that you and I are perfect as we are and that others will just have to "put up with us" because "that's the way God made us!" Our creation gifts can be intensified and expanded as we offer them up to the Lord. By His grace, hidden talents can be released and significant healing experienced to enable us to grow so that the fruits of God's Spirit can be more fully expressed through our personalities.

What Are Your Creation Gifts?

The four basic creation gifts in the area of personality are thinking, feeling, intuiting, and sensing. It all depends on your favorite mental process. If you are interested in how the theory determines your favorite function—your beginning gift—you will want to study the relevant pages in Myers' book.[2] I have also included an explanation at the back of this book to guide you in understanding your favorite mental function. The illustration on page 36 will help you to locate your special creation gift.

This basic gift is the most important aspect of your personality type. It is likely that aspect of yourself which you most wish others understood. It is the lens through which you look at life. It is the compass by which you navigate. This favorite mental process is extroverted by Extroverts, but is introverted by Introverts. This means that you will be more likely to observe an Extrovert's "beginning gift" but will need to get to know the Introvert before realizing the nature of his or her "internal chairperson of the board" which directs everything.

Let's take a closer look at each of these four basic gifts and notice the distinctive shapes and colorations which they bring to our personalities. In each of my summaries I have attempted to be faithful to the descriptions given by Myers, while interpreting and illustrating them from my own experience.

✠ *Sensing.* If you are a member of one of the four sensing types, your creation gift has to do with the way you are tuned in to things around you. You probably appreciate the things of

Finding Your Favorite Function

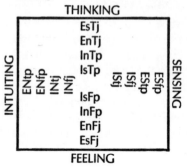

this planet and enjoy its pleasures and beauty. You care about your surroundings. You have an eye for details, whether in personal appearance or in things pertaining to your work. You value accuracy and order. You live in the here and now. For you, the present moment can be a sacrament of the Lord's presence, because you experience Him in and through the ordinary things of life—through people, events, and nature.

But you are also well aware that you can get earthbound and that present enjoyment and immediate security can become as chains, binding you and hindering your movement when God calls you to venture forth into some unknown or untried situation. And since you are attracted to what can be seen, felt, touched, smelled, and tasted, you may sometimes find it difficult to make sacrifices for the intangible realities of life.

✠ *Intuiting.* If you are one of the four intuitive personality types, you are blessed with the creation gift of imagination. Because of it, you are never quite satisfied with things as they are. You seem to be inexorably drawn toward what could be, lured by the dream of the future's possibilities. Because of your deep-seated confidence in such visions, you probably are willing to sacrifice for your dreams. For you, today is a stepping-stone into tomorrow. You live by inspiration, and you need to be ignited by vision and sustained by fresh glimpses of that vision and by the joy of achievements which reinforce your conviction about the possibility of the "not yet." Your enthusiasm may be so contagious that you are able to persuade others to follow your dreams.

But you are also aware of your inadequacies. You may feel that details bog you down. Sometimes you may spin castles in the air and your plans lack sufficient grounding in the facts. Your hopes for tomorrow may cause you to miss the precious moments of today—the changing seasons, or the stages of your child's growth. Unsatisfied with things as they are, you may feel a sense of restlessness which others see as evidence of a changeable, perhaps even unpredictable, nature.

✠ *Thinking.* If you find yourself in one of the four personality types in this group, you experience the creation gift of critical thinking. You are probably compelled to look for the truth and to understand it, if not communicate it. You may develop skills in logic and have the ability to dissect matters, testing out their constituent elements. You organize what you see, categorize it, and sum it all up. With efficiency of expression, you highlight the salient points and state your own conclusions succinctly and as matters of fact. You are a problem solver and have the skills of a technician, either in theoretical matters or in practical things.

But from time to time you may be painfully aware of your weak side as well. Your logical and analytical approach to things may come across as cold and calculating to others who feel alienated from you. Even though you may be right, you may find yourself being avoided and your ideas resisted.

✠ *Feeling.* If you are one of the four feeling types, you evidence the creation gift of empathy or compassion. Your people skills are valuable, and your knack for diplomacy may have helped in delicate situations more than once. You are naturally friendly and, whether you are reserved or outgoing, you probably communicate warmth to others. You may not know where to begin, what to exclude, or when to stop when you share with others, but sharing is probably important to you because of your relational nature.

But you may have also become aware of some of your serious gaps. You may tend to sweep conflict under the rug; your need to preserve harmony through delicate tactfulness may make it difficult for you to be straightforward and absolutely truthful. Because of your sensitivity to feelings (your own and those of others), you may not be terribly efficient and could find yourself often derailed from important tasks by personal concerns. Your deep feelings about situations sometimes cloud your ability to think about things with objectivity. At times you may find yourself taking something personally, only to discover later that it wasn't intended to be received in that way at all.

What Infirmities Do You Carry in Your Personality?

The Apostle Paul used a helpful word to speak of our weaknesses. He called them infirmities (Romans 8:26, KJV). Our infirmities are not sins, but their origin can be traced back to the fall of Adam and Eve in the Garden of Eden (Genesis 3:14-21). The intended harmony of life was disrupted by the initial disobedience of our first parents. That original sin, though forgiven, produced enduring consequences in every dimension of our lives: spiritual, physical, relational, material. For example: now our circumstances can become testing, our relationships trying, and our human efforts very tiring. Such "facts of life" have issued from the disruption of all Creation. This disruption has increased the resistances which we must face and has decreased our capacities for handling them.

An infirmity always has to do with the inability to produce the results which we desire, because of our own human limitations. In 2 Corinthians 12, the Apostle Paul spoke of his "thorn in the flesh" which had not been taken away, even though he had prayed for relief three times. He recognized that God had a purpose for not removing it. Its presence kept him humbly depending on God's resources to see him through.

> And He said to me, "My grace is sufficient for you, for My strength is made perfect in weakness." Therefore most gladly I will rather boast in my infirmities, that the power of Christ may rest upon me. Therefore I take pleasure in infirmities ... for Christ's sake. For when I am weak, then I am strong.
>
> 2 Corinthians 12:9-10

Experiences which make us aware of our weaknesses can become occasions for fresh recognition of our utter dependence upon the Lord!

When we speak of personality, we must talk not only about giftedness but also about infirmities. You noticed in the descriptions of the four creation gifts that each one has its weak side. It is important to remember that while many weaknesses come from our personality types, these infirmities are not sins. They do, however, predispose us for certain kinds of failings and can become occasions for sin. You may have noticed that many of the sins which you often need to confess come from your "weak side." It is only reasonable that when the evil one attacks, he chooses to hit us at our most vulnerable spot!

Your Personality Type Does Not Define the Boundaries of Your Being!

While personality type is a gift to be donated to God for His purposes, it is by no means a definition of the boundaries of being! The history of the church is filled with examples of persons who found themselves thrust into situations which caused them to reach down deep and draw upon the spiritual resources which God supplied within them and the special resources of His body, the church, around them. This gave them the power to rise to challenges and to do things and respond in ways which they might ordinarily have avoided.

Spirituality does not mean taking the path of least resistance or always doing what is most comfortable or what comes most naturally. Christ spoke about how we must be willing to die to self-will and to offer ourselves up to cooperate with the Lord. This means that sometimes the Extrovert will have to surrender the desire to do all the talking and give others the space they need. Sometimes the Introvert will have to sacrifice the preference for solitude and become actively involved in some ministry. Whenever we do respond to God's call in such ways, we experience growth and transcendence. We discover that we can be more through Christ than we could ever have been if left to ourselves!

Your Personality Type Impacts Your Devotional Style

While God may speak directly to the human spirit, He most often seems to make use of the receptive apparatus of our minds and personalities in order to communicate Himself to us. At first, your creation gift may be your best wavelength for communication with God through prayer and meditation. You may have instinctively discovered this as you have grown in Christ. Or, you may be struggling to make some devotional pattern work for you just because it has worked for someone else you respect who had recommended it to you. If you are searching for ways of vitalizing your relationship with God, the application of some new realizations about your personality may provide an important key. We'll look at some of those possibilities in the pages ahead. We will also note how to deal with the one-sidedness and dullness which can seep into the spiritual life, simply because we are not being stretched in the directions where we need to grow.

I mentioned above that at first our creation gift may give us the clue as to our best wavelength for the cultivation of our devotional life. However, many of us have experienced another phenomenon. At some point along the way, perhaps at mid-life, we become open in some rather new ways to God. The sensing person may have powerful and spiritually meaningful dreams. The intuitive person begins to need sensory experiences to recharge spiritually, and so forth. We are discovering that our weak side is becoming our important new channel through which the Lord is refreshing our lives. This leads us to the whole idea of growth.

Growth toward Wholeness

I believe that there is within each of us a Spirit-induced drive toward wholeness. In chapter 1, we saw a picture of such wholeness in Jesus. Through our attachment to Him and in the midst of the pressures and opportunities of life, we can grow more mature.

The most fruitful place of growth for those in the second half of life is in the area which is the polar opposite to their creation gift—the "weak side" is really a kind of inner "buried treasure." If you are a thinker, then it is the area of feeling. If you are an intuitive person, it is the sensing dimension, and so forth.

This may become the domain in which you find yourself blindsided by breakthrough experiences of God's truth, beauty, love, and light. Such encounters are not programmable by us; we must simply remain faithful and open to the Father. However, we may well discover that spiritual exercises which mine our buried treasure may surface surprising discoveries of God's grace. More about that later!

You Are the Only You God Ever Made

In the first chapter we began with the question, "Does God change a person's personality?" For some of us the discovery and celebration of our creation gifts is a truly liberating experience. We have finally "come home" to the fact that we don't have to be like anyone else. It is a joyful breakthrough to finally realize that when we offer to the Lord the self that we are, He can convey His grace through us in His own special ways. It just may be possible that God can manifest facets of His light through your soul which He could never display through anyone else in quite the same way.

It is just as liberating a discovery when we accept the fact that we are not bound up in the box of our creation gift, but that through our willing sacrifice of self-will, and by our utter reliance upon the resources of God within us and the body of Christ around us, He can help us grow and make us sufficient for the situations in which He places us.

> I have strength for all things in Christ who empowers me—I am ready for anything and equal to anything through Him who infuses inner strength into me, [that is, I am self-sufficient in Christ's sufficiency].
>
> Philippians 4:13, AMP

On the next page is a prayer exercise. It is designed so that the four instructions engage you with each dimension—sensing, intuition, thinking, and feeling. You are encouraged to take some time at the conclusion of each chapter to open yourself to God and allow Him to minister to you through this period of prayer.

The Second Touch

*Then He put His hands on his eyes again and made him
look up. And he was restored and saw everyone clearly.*

Mark 8:25

———————————— ■ ————————————

Read Mark 8:22-26 aloud. Close your eyes and visualize the
story in as vivid detail as possible, with all of your senses fully
engaged.

Imagine yourself being brought to Jesus by someone who
prays for you. What blindness in you is in need of His second
touch? Envision the way He treats you and speaks to you.

Allow Christ to help you understand about this blindness, its
sources and manifestations. Consider what healing involves
and how Christ is accomplishing it in you. What cooperation is
needed from you?

Linger silently in Jesus' presence, while His hand rests on
your shoulder.

Chapter Three

The Energizers

ESTP and ESFP

The Energizers' presence may be aptly described as a "force field" which pervades the room. People find themselves propelled along by their action or magnetized by their storytelling. Energizers are enjoyable to be with because they exude camaraderie and an enthusiasm for life. When their gifts are offered up to God, they can become powerful witnesses for Christ and trusted peacemakers in His body.

Case Study: David

We would be hard-pressed to find any biblical character who displays so many of the Energizers' traits as does David. This winsome figure dominates the screen in four great books of the Old Testament: 1 and 2 Samuel, 1 Chronicles, and the Book of Psalms, to which he was the principal contributor. From the large body of material available, I have selected those portions of his story which are most illustrative of this personality type.

✠ *Action and energy.* From the beginning David is described as handsome and "ruddy," a man of the out-of-doors, brimming with energy. We are told of his exploits as a young shepherd, his daring challenge to Goliath, his fugitive years of successfully eluding Saul, his heroics as a guerrilla leader, and his magnificent years as king. He consolidated an empire in the midst of hostile forces, built a capital city, survived a coup led by his own son, and all the while was writing scores of spiritual songs and poems, many of which appear in our Book of Psalms. David was a man of action and, as such, typifies a chief characteristic of those we are calling the Energizers.

✠ *Skill and style.* Here was a man who possessed boundless energy and exhibited great physical skill and deftness. He seemed to use slingshot, harp, and sword as extensions of his being. His dance before the ark of the covenant was no one-two-three step; he was "leaping and whirling before the Lord with all his might." In fact, this was done with such unabashed abandon that his wife had a few things to say to him about it! He was as skillful in the social and political arenas as in the physical. He seemed to know when to make the decisive move and when to hold back. Scripture informs us that what may have appeared to be perfectly spontaneous was, in fact, due to his sensitivity to the Lord from whom he often sought very specific direction.

✠ *Practicality and adaptability.* David's practical nature is often evident in his story. While not an unprincipled man, he could determine what expediency demanded and quickly adapt to his changing circumstances. He didn't think twice about deceiving the good priest Ahimelech and working around the rules, justifying why he and his hungry men could be fed with the showbread from off the altar of God (1 Samuel 21:1-6).

After repeated attempts at reconciliation, David realized that one day he would die at Saul's hand if he didn't take appropriate action, so he struck a deal with the enemy and was given a country village as a base of operations for his rebel band. Then when the Philistine commander, Achish, told David that he expected David and his men to join him in battle against Saul, David was capable of shrewd deception as demonstrated by his cryptic nonreply, "Surely you know what your servant can do" (1 Samuel 28:2). David had the capacity to read situations and adapt to realities as he met them.

✠ *Friendship and generosity.* The story of David is one of great loyalties and deep friendships. He and Saul's son, Jonathan, were bound together in a bond which endured even after Jonathan's death. Another of Saul's children, Michal, devoted her life to David rather than to her father.

David's "mighty men" were the 400 who joined his guerrilla camp at the cave of Adullam when "everyone who was in distress, everyone who was in debt, and everyone who was discontented gathered to him. So he became captain over them" (1 Samuel 22:2). This ragtag lot became his core group and fought with him throughout his career. Their commitment to David is one of the great military stories of all time.

One glimpse of their loyalty is caught in 1 Chronicles 11. The Philistines had Bethlehem, David's childhood home. David was in hiding in the hills. His men overheard him lament, "Oh, that someone would give me a drink of water from the well of Bethlehem!" (v. 17) Three of his men slipped out under the cover of darkness, broke through the Philistine camp and returned with a skin full of water for their beloved leader. When David realized what they had done, he wouldn't drink the water, but poured it out as an offering to the Lord. He realized the price the men had been willing to pay because of their love for him, and he knew that only God was worthy of such devotion!

✠ *Toleration and openness.* One stands amazed at David's "toleration quotient." Just how many times would he forgive Saul or his own treacherous son, Absalom? Page after page the stories unfold, each showing David still trying to bring reconciliation, not wishing physical harm on his mortal enemies. One of these was the scoundrel, Shimei. When David was having to evacuate Jerusalem because of Absalom's impending march on that city, Shimei came out cursing David, kicking dirt on him and throwing stones, gleefully announcing that David's overthrow was just what he deserved. King David could have had Shimei's head on a platter; instead he tolerated the abuse, realizing that the Lord was allowing it for some purpose and might even bring forth good from it! Later, when David's fortunes were restored and he was marching back to Jerusalem, who should greet him at the river but Shimei—full of apologies and asking for mercy. And David received him with grace! Such is the kind of openness you learn to expect from an Energizer!

✠ *Gullibility and corruptibility.* Of course, this leads to the observation that David was susceptible to seduction. That he would believe Shimei's insincere penitence is only one instance. He was almost naive in the way he trusted Absalom who was stealing the throne right out from under him, over several years. His credulity is also seen in his response to a man named Ziba who maliciously maligned his master, Mephibosheth, who had been almost as a son to David. David was vulnerable to physical seduction as well. The tragic story of Bathsheba and Uriah illustrates this fact poignantly enough.

The Energizer's Creation Gifts

David gives us the flavor of the Energizer's personality traits. Alliteration may help us identify the creation gifts which God has given to this group. We will describe them with six "A's": action, altruism, adaptability, acceptance, ardor, and appreciation for beauty. While each of these words may not describe every Energizer, taken together they do typify the group.[1]

✠ *Action.* Energizers live in the now and savor every minute of it! They love life and know how to get the most from it. They don't want to miss anything, and so may spread themselves thin. Very often their interests have a physical quality to them, with sports and outdoor activities having a special appeal. If they aren't involved *doing* things, they are likely to be found entertaining others with the stories of their adventures and exploits. Many Energizers seem to be born performers.

✠ *Altruism.* Energizers delight in rising to the occasion, coming to the rescue, and giving freely of themselves and their possessions in order to meet another's genuine need. They are especially motivated to respond when there is a call for urgent action. But if the other person simply needs the gift of presence or a listening ear, an Energizer may have to exert a special effort of will strengthened by grace, because such a "passive" response is not easy. Energizers are better at rising to the challenge of a crisis than dealing with long-term situations like lengthy illness or apparently irresolvable troubles.

Such experiences may tend to frustrate them, since they may feel that there is nothing that they can do to produce a change for the better.

They enjoy breadth of relationships and having lots of friends, rather than focusing deeply on just a few. This sometimes comes as a disappointing surprise to their acquaintances, who may misinterpret the Energizer's charm and friendliness for devotion and singleheartedness.

✠ *Adaptability.* Isabel Briggs Myers called Energizers "adaptable realists."[2] Rather than coming to a situation with a ready-made solution, they prefer to "read" the situation, paying attention to their experiences of things and people in order to uncover some inherent way of resolving a problem.

A teacher who possesses this quality might prepare lesson plans very differently than one who would never think of entering the classroom without a detailed agenda. The Energizer's preparation could assume the form of gathering materials and accumulating strategies from which selections can be made on the spot, in light of the unfolding dynamics of the class. Energizers often exhibit the ability to read those dynamics with an uncanny eye! They would much rather be resourceful than programmed in their approach.

Energizers do not feel bound by standard ways of doing things. They tend to interpret rules broadly in the light of changing situations, adapting them to fit the need of an occasion. This quality frustrates those who prefer a narrow interpretation of the rules! Expediency and pragmatism are more characteristic of Energizers than strictness and conformity.

✠ *Acceptance.* Energizers often exhibit a remarkable level of toleration and can be amazingly accepting of people. In our case study, David showed such a quality in the way he dealt with his enemies. This quality probably emerges from their willingness to take others as they find them, rather than approaching them with firm and fixed expectations to which they ought to measure up. Such a relaxed and accepting manner enables them to bring a great measure of peaceability and goodwill into otherwise tense situations. As a result, they often have a reconciling ministry in a group where there are opposing factions.

Energizer parents will probably show this same relaxed openness to their children that they demonstrate to others. Their children will probably experience a significant amount of freedom, while remaining aware of the accountability which their Energizer parents expect from them.

✠ *Ardor.* Energizers approach life with a certain flair, fervor, and intensity. They tend to enjoy whatever they are doing and do it with all their heart. Everything becomes a game for them. This is not to say that they take things lightly, for they do not. They simply meet life with wholehearted enthusiasm.

✠ *Appreciation.* Finally, Energizers appreciate the good things of life. Their senses are fully alive and they thoroughly enjoy the sounds of good music, the taste of delicious food, the texture of rich wood, the look of nice clothes. Such experiences are invigorating and refreshing to them. They may also be impressed by persons who are attractive, have nice things, dress in a becoming manner, or have fine taste.

Scripture says that when David was selected by Samuel as the king apparent, the guiding light for Samuel was that "man looks on the outward appearance, but the Lord looks on the heart." In young David, He saw one whose heart was right. However, because of personality type, David himself *could* be swayed by outward appearances. Sometimes this got him into trouble. Let's turn now to the infirmities of the Energizer.

The Energizer's Infirmities

The Energizer's *sensing* approach to life, while contributing to the special gifts which they bring, also has its weak elements. Here are some of the vulnerabilities which, although not inevitable, may be part of the Energizer's spiritual struggle.

✠ *Allurement and seduction.* David seemed particularly vulnerable to feminine beauty. Bathsheba was practically irresistible, so taken was he by her appearance. The sensual attraction of shape, fragrance, and touch bore the promise of such pleasure that David went to incredible lengths to possess Bathsheba. So fired were his passions that he ultimately devised an intricate plot to have her husband, Uriah, killed in battle.

Energizers need to anticipate the power of physical attractions and at the same time remember these words from the Book of Hebrews:

> We do not have a High Priest who cannot sympathize with our weaknesses, but was in all points tempted as we are, yet without sin. Let us therefore come boldly to the throne of grace, that we may obtain mercy and find grace to help in time of need. Hebrews 4:15-16

Physical seduction can take forms other than sexual allurement. It might also be experienced by the appeal of material possessions, a proneness to judge by outward appearances, or a craving for excitement, stimulation, or entertainment.

Seduction is often accompanied by its insidious ally, self-deception. This internal hypocrisy was perhaps the very root of David's corruptibility. One remarkable aspect of the Bathsheba/Uriah story is that God gave David about twelve months before sending the Prophet Nathan to confront David with his sinful deed. Twelve months and apparently David never lifted up his heart to God for forgiveness! One wonders what rationalizations, self-justifications, and excuses David was making in order to insulate himself from his guilt. Energizers need to be alert to any tendency toward such self-deception, and also to cultivate a transparent spirit before the Lord.

✠ *Brinkmanship and self-aggrandizement.* Energizers love a crisis and may feel that they are at their best when having to rise to the occasion. In the heat of the action, they may feel most alive. Since emergencies meet important ego needs, they may be tempted (even unconsciously) to create such events if they do not naturally encounter them. Brinkmanship can be defined as pursuing a dangerous policy to the far limit of safety. Such a courting of disaster may be invigorating to an Energizer, but it is unhealthy for, and unnerving to, others around them. The importance of this in family matters is obvious!

Since the Energizer not only enjoys the action but also loves to tell about it when it is over, there is another closely allied temptation — making a display of oneself. It should be remembered that while courage is a virtue, making a show of courage, or of any grace or gift, is not.

Self-aggrandizement is the desire to increase one's stature in the eyes of others, especially by parading achievements or displaying possessions. It was a dark day, indeed, when David disobeyed the Lord's specific command that there be no census taken of the kingdom. Apparently the desire to enhance his image among his people led David to proceed with the census. He may have thought that if the nation really saw the full measure of his "success," by realizing the amazingly large number of persons in the kingdom, they would come to appreciate his greatness even more. However, as soon as the tally was reported, David fell under a deep conviction of his prideful sin.

Bravado has the effect of separating one from others. Prideful self-elevation not only fails to celebrate solidarity in community, but also fails to credit the One who is the true Source of our gifts. Sensitivity to this form of personal pride may be critical to the Energizer's spiritual growth.

✠ *Expediency and opportunism.* Energizers have the adroitness to adapt themselves to changing circumstances. However, the flip side of this is that by habitually opting for pragmatic solutions, they often fail to develop deep commitments to those unchanging principles which produce a sense of stability and develop a quality of faithfulness in their lives.[3]

Natural Ways for Energizers to Nurture Faith

The nurture of the Energizer's faith will, especially in the early stages of growth, depend largely upon the sensory path.

✠ *Physical spirituality.* This group will fully appreciate the physical side of the spiritual life. Through the sights and sounds of the out-of-doors, they will experience the magnificent grandeur and marvelous power of the Lord. Fresh air and exercise will aid their devotion. These are the people who, when they go to a church retreat, are most bewildered that so much time is spent indoors in brainwork, practically excluding any time to enjoy the glory of the natural surroundings to which they have retreated. Theirs is a sensual spirituality. Often God's grace is experienced profoundly through their five senses.

✠ *A spirituality of service.* Their practical approach to life will demand that devotion result in concrete action for others. Their native generosity and delight in coming to the aid of others gives their spiritual expression a very down-to-earth quality. In fact, if they do not have such channels for ministry, they tend to feel increasingly distant from God. The renewal of their spiritual vitality will often come through their active ministry.

A friend of mine who is an Energizer came for a visit to our home. On Sunday he attended the church I was pastoring at the time. After the service he said, "Do you know the part of the service where I really felt God?" I secretly hoped that he would say that it had been my sermon! But he answered, "The announcements!" Somewhat stunned, I asked him what he meant. He replied, "When you were reminding the congregation of the schedule for the week, I realized how much these people were doing for others. That's where God is for me!"

Eventually, many Energizers will long for balance in their lives. The person who has been furiously active will begin hungering for quiet. As the senses feel overloaded, there will come a desire to slow down the constant flood of experience in order to simply "be." To nurture such balance, it is important for Energizers to exercise the daily discipline of prayer, and to discover the reality of God's presence within, rather than constantly seeking Him without. They need the power of the Word to help them form those deep commitments to enduring principles which will give stability to their lives. They need the quiet cultivation of Christ's companionship in order to keep themselves on course with firm purpose and deep resolve in the face of the changing winds of circumstance.

The Energizer's Path toward Wholeness

✠ *Affirm your gifts.* As with all personality types, the Energizers must learn to appreciate and celebrate God's creation gifts. They can grow in this sense of affirmation as they consciously make the connection between their endless variety of experiences and the many expressions of God's providence. Through praying over your experiences, you will come to recognize the relationship between worship and action, and will grow in the realization that this life which you love is first and foremost a "graced life."

To foster such an awareness, David turned his experiences into psalms. Read Psalm 51 in light of David's moral failure, or Psalm 18 in light of God's protection from his mortal enemies. Such prayer-poems as these became the means by which the scatteredness of his life was unified and his brokenness healed. In David, we encounter a man of profound spiritual depth blended with personal vitality.

✠ *Deny your self-will.* It is not unusual in a forest to see trees which have been identified with a red slash. They are marked for cutting. But the cutting has a purpose. Perhaps it is to halt the spread of a disease or to build an access road. Likewise, there may be areas of an Energizer's life which are marked out by the Lord for His own purposes. Perhaps He will ask you to sacrifice some action in preference for reflection. He might ask you to hand over your desire for an exciting challenge to remain faithful at an exacting duty. Or He may ask you to reduce some of your commitments in order to cultivate certain relationships.

At the end of his life, David was seeking to renew his relationship with God. He was told to erect an altar to the Lord at a certain site. When he arrived there, the man who owned the place offered to *give* David everything he needed—the place for the altar, oxen for the sacrifice, and various implements which he could break up and use for firewood. David's answer reminds us of the necessity of sacrifice in the interest of spiritual growth. "No," he said to the free offer, "but I will surely buy it from you for a price; nor will I offer burnt offerings to the Lord my God with that which costs me nothing" (2 Samuel 24:24).

From Fear to Faith

The Lord is my light and my salvation; whom shall I fear? The Lord is the strength of my life; of whom shall I be afraid? Psalm 27:1

Sing a hymn or chorus based on this psalm. Let your finger guide your eyes as you read Psalm 27:1-9; allow your touch to pause upon those words which hold special meaning for you.

When was some fear of yours dissipated by the light? Picture the kind of refuge where you would feel most secure. Pray verses 1 and 2 with these images in mind.

Make lists of the action words and feeling words in these verses. Think of the relationship between the two lists. How is fear replaced by confidence?

Talk to Christ about your specific fears. Allow the psalmist's words to become your personal prayer.

Chapter Four

The Stabilizers
ISTJ and ISFJ

These persons are like the Rock of Gibraltar — steady, reliable, and dependable; they are the Stabilizers among us. They respect and honor tradition and are concerned that we be faithful to our history. They are marked by their measured, meticulous, and observant manner. It makes sense that when the church was young and the Gospel was spreading like a prairie fire, God might select a person with such qualities to be the first to collect, record, and preserve the essential stories which were used to teach the truth of Christ.

Case Study: Mark

We are limited in our knowledge of the details of Mark's life. We know that his mother's name was Mary, and that she was apparently a widow when the events of the Book of Acts took place. Wealthy enough to have a large house, Mary welcomed the Jerusalem Christians to her home for their regular worship, even in times of persecution. When Peter was released from prison, he knew exactly where to find his sisters and brothers in Christ — at the house where Mary and her son Mark lived. Paul selected Mark to be the administrative assistant for his first missionary journey. Although there was a misunderstanding during that journey and they parted company, they came back together in later years for other special mission projects.

It is from Papias, an early church historian, that we learn of Mark's work as an author.

> Mark, indeed, having been the interpreter of Peter, wrote accurately, howbeit not in order, all that he recalled of what was either said or done by the Lord. For he neither heard the Lord, nor was he a follower of His, but, at a later date [he learned from] . . . Peter, who used to adapt his instructions to the needs of the moment, but not with a view to putting together the Dominical oracles in orderly fashion: so that Mark did no wrong in thus writing some things as he recalled them. For he kept a single aim in view: not to omit anything of what he heard, nor to state anything herein falsely.[1]

From this interesting statement and from the actual composition of the Gospel of Mark, we can observe some important characteristics of a Stabilizer.

✣ *Factuality and simplicity.* The days of active ministry for those who had been eyewitnesses to Christ were rapidly passing. Age and martyrdom were reducing their number. It became increasingly important that the recollections of the apostles be recorded for posterity. Their teachings about Jesus were the very foundation of the church. Their oral reports needed to be transferred to parchment so that there would be written documents from which faith could be fed. As a friend and assistant of the Apostle Peter, Mark realized the importance of this very practical task and understood his own unique position to respond. God's call was upon him.

Papias noted that Mark had the capacity to remember details. He could recall the many stories which he had heard Peter tell so often. Those stories had not been told for entertainment, but for instruction. In the process they had become simplified, honed, and distilled to their essentials. Mark not only remembered them but also recorded those recollections. His record is marked by its simplicity and directness, and was unembellished by his own commentary or reflections. He gave a straightforward accounting of what he had heard from Peter, and wrote under the guidance of the Spirit working through his personality. The simplicity, factuality, and straightforwardness so characteristic of Mark are inherent in Stabilizers.

✠ *Realism and concreteness.* While Mark's Gospel is un- adorned, its power seems to lie in its realism and concrete- ness. Mark preserved history by writing with the quality of an eyewitness reporter. He did not fail to record the rich, sensory details which had grabbed him when he first heard these sto- ries. He often included more of these realistic touches than either Matthew or Luke when they wrote about the same events. For example, he remembered that when the Lord's disciples tried to stop people from bringing children to Jesus for Him to bless them, Jesus became *angry*. After Jesus' re- sponse to them about the importance of receiving the kingdom as a little child, He *took the children in His arms, placed His hands on each of them, and blessed them*. These are details which give concreteness to the event, but which the other Gospel writers did not include. It is just such realism and down-to-earthness, so characteristic of Stabilizers, which oc- curs page after page in Mark's Gospel.

✠ *Methodical organization and creative practicality.* The very way that Mark organized his material is worth noting. Unlike the other Gospel writers, he gathered units of material according to their type (parables, for example) or linked stories together with the use of a key word or theme. We see an example of this latter style in Mark 8, where the theme of blindness and sight becomes the thread drawing several pieces of material together. The Pharisees are blind to the signs of the kingdom and ask for proof (8:11ff); the disciples have eyes to see but do not grasp who Jesus really is (8:14ff); at Bethsai- da Jesus gives a blind man a "second touch" after which he sees "everyone clearly" (8:22ff); immediately thereafter we are told that Peter finally recognized Jesus' true identity, an- nouncing, "You are the Christ" (8:27ff). Many scholars believe that Mark's distinctive methodical organization was intended as a memory aid. He was assisting the Christian teachers who would be turning to his writings as a source book for their ministry, memorizing chunks of his Gospel for retelling to others. Mark's method was a stroke of creative practicality. He was making such memorization easier for them. System and method and creative practicality, so common to Stabilizers, are visible in this Gospel.

The Stabilizer's Creation Gifts

Let's turn now to a review of the special qualities and traits which are common to Stabilizers.[2]

✠ *Thoroughness and persistence.* Stabilizers can be painstakingly thorough in their work. They also appreciate exactness and precision in the work of others. They have a capacity for remembering details, especially those with personal meaning. For example, a Stabilizer may not be able to tell you exactly the color of the wall of the hallway leading to his office, but he will be able to tell you where every report has been filed and precisely where he has placed all of the materials which are important to his job.

Stabilizers tend to be meticulous and painstaking and are often remarkably persistent in their pursuit of a project or task. They look upon it as a duty or personal responsibility which they must fulfill for the benefit of the family, the organization, or the company.

✠ *Practicality and prudence.* They are practical in their interests and seem more like technicians than theoreticians. They have less interest in speculation, preferring instead to see how something will be applied and what it will actually do. In an organization, the Stabilizers can become easily frustrated with those who love to speculate, "What if we . . ." because the Stabilizers immediately begin mentally translating others' brainstorms into action plans and to-do lists, with a view to the practical consequences and concrete implications not only for the organization, but for themselves as well. Sometimes they can become overwhelmed and feel swamped in brainstorming or blue-sky sessions. At such meetings, others—especially Crusaders and Renewers—might be speculating about various untried procedures or uncharted possibilities which might be explored. Meanwhile, the Stabilizers are mentally calculating project costs, anticipating the many possible flaws in the plans, and making lists of all of the data which would have to be amassed in order to assess the realism of the intuitives' dreams. Then, before they have begun to assimilate it all, someone else has spun out yet another idea, and then another!

One Stabilizer remarked, "People with creative imaginations may think that we are their enemies and that we are against what they want to do. Actually, we may want to arrive at the same goal ourselves, but we want to be able to feel secure about getting there."

Stabilizers seem to have a built-in caution light when it comes to change. They have a sense of continuity with the past and appreciate all the efforts others have made to bring us to where we are now. They treasure traditions, and feel an obligation to observe and preserve them out of respect and honor for our heritage. For this reason they are careful about breaking with tradition, setting new precedents, or launching into untried ways. They may have particular difficulties with Crusaders— extrovertive intuitives—who approach life so very differently.

Stabilizers are creative persons, but always in a very practical way. We noted Mark's ingenious way of organizing his Gospel with memory devices to aid teachers. It is not unusual for a Stabilizer to come up with a way of organizing materials or devising routines for handling repetitive tasks which is marked by its simplicity and at the same time is beautifully practical.

Stabilizers are unlikely to leave any stone unturned in their efforts to complete their projects. In fact, their concentration on fine points may strike those of other personality types as "obsessive." It is important for others not to judge them harshly at this point, but to appreciate the personal sense of responsibility which Stabilizers shoulder in their work.

✠ *Dependability and common sense.* The sense of personal obligation to which we have just alluded, and their commitment to continuing the traditions and perpetuating our institutions, give the Stabilizers their quality of bedrock dependability. They can be counted on to finish what they start. When no one else can be found to take on some task, they will often rise to the occasion—especially if they see the task as a way of carrying into the future what we have received from the past.

Their demeanor is businesslike, and they seem unflappable, regardless of the situation. This stable, outward countenance contributes to the confidence which others feel in their abilities.

A lady who is an Energizer once remarked to me, "All this time I've been wanting our pastor (a Stabilizer) to be more spontaneous. Now I realize that our personalities are just different. He communicates stability and that is really important. Both ways are important — openness and stability, enthusiasm and reserve."

Stabilizers bring this same quality of dependability into family life. Their commitments to their spouses are deep. Rules and expectations will be made clear to their children. Consistency will characterize their disciplining.

However, Myers reminds us that when Stabilizers know you well and trust you, you may be given a peek into their other side. There you may be surprised by their delightful twists of humor and their entertaining personal reactions to things going on around them. This is an especially endearing quality to those who are privileged to experience it.[3]

The Stabilizer's Infirmities

We will treat three sets of weaknesses to which Stabilizers may be especially susceptible.

✠ *Self-absorption and hiddenness.* If Stabilizers have insufficiently developed either their thinking or feeling functions, they can become locked into themselves. Without the outlet of clear communication to others, they can become absorbed in private reactions to their own personal impressions.[4] If this happens, their important gifts are essentially unavailable to those around them. Mark could have been completely immersed in the things which he was seeing and hearing; fortunately for us, he was committed to communicating his observations to others. A woman may have a powerfully retentive mind, the capacity to compare fact with fact and to remember tradition with reverence; but if she is unable to elucidate her observations or is hesitant to engage with others, the group will never have the benefit of her vital gifts.

✠ *Suspicion and prudishness.* We have already noted the difficulty which Stabilizers may have with Crusaders. Because of their high regard for tradition and their conservative nature in the face of change, their gift of prudence may degenerate into prudishness and their sensibility dissolve into suspicion.[5]

Because they do not trust their own intuitions, they tend to view intuitive persons with similar distrust. Since their relatively undeveloped intuitive capacity is their least used ability, it may still be relatively immature. So when their intuition does surge into consciousness in some unguarded moment, it often carries with it a sense of foreboding, generating a fear of dark and sinister prospects for the future.[6] When Stabilizers are verbalizing these intuitions, others may regard them as negative doomsayers, alarmists undermining confidence, and depressing to be around.

Considering the Stabilizers' suspicion of intuitive vision, the following bit of wisdom may be important for them to remember.

> It would be good to be able to say that we should dispense with visions entirely and deal only with reality. But that may be the most utopian vision of all. Reality is far too complex to be comprehended by any given mind. Visions are like maps that guide us through a tangle of bewildering complexities ... visions are indispensable—but dangerous, precisely to the extent that we confuse them with reality itself.[7]

It is important for Stabilizers to learn to cultivate their own intuitive capacities until they are less fearful of them.

✠ *Idolatry and protectionism.* Because of their tendency to lock in on their own personal perceptions about the nature of reality, it is tempting for Stabilizers to think that their perceptions are the only correct ways of seeing things. This attitude can become a breeding ground for arrogance, as it feeds on idolization of their own thoughts or systems.

Natural Ways for Stabilizers to Nourish Faith

What are some important ways by which Stabilizers can nurture their spiritual life?

✠ *Quietness.* Since by nature people in this personality group have to process so much outside stimulation, they may sometimes experience a sensory overload and feel a special need for a quiet place to which they can withdraw from all the outward distractions. There, away from the constant chatter of the television or the ringing of the phone, they will be more able to focus themselves, consider their experiences, and sort things out.

✠ *Structured prayer.* Their predisposition for method and routine may make structured prayer a helpful discipline. One Stabilizer I know has a book on his desk into which he retreats each morning before beginning the day's work. It is John Bailey's classic *A Diary of Private Prayer.* It provides both structure and meaningful content to guide his morning devotions.

If you are a Stabilizer, you might experiment with an even more extensive devotional structure as, for example, a notebook with eight dividers relating to the eight components of the Lord's Prayer. Each morning or evening, you would take each section in sequence, praying with the pattern given by the Lord.

"Our Father" leads you to a daily prayer of adoration to the Trinity.

"Hallowed be Thy name" reminds you to give thanks for concrete expressions of God's goodness surrounding you.

"Thy kingdom come" introduces a time for intercession. This section might contain a list of persons and situations for which you pray, including those beyond your circle of intimate friends and relatives, so that you will remember to pray for the homeless, oppressed, and persecuted.

"Thy will be done" brings you to a section of supplications recorded in the notebook. These include desires, decisions, and special needs about which you need to pray.

"Give us this day our daily bread" is a simple prayer of openness and surrender before your time of meditation on God's Word.

"And forgive us our trespasses" leads you to a period of self-examination and confession.

"As we forgive those who trespass against us" reminds you to pray specifically for your enemies and about your own attitudes toward them.

"And lead us not into temptation" is the final section of the notebook, calling you to the day ahead with its own special tests and difficulties. It is a time of anticipatory prayer for grace to help in time of need, and a place where you will note insights or reminders which have come through prayer.

I have given this format in its entirety, since it may be suggestive of other ways of structuring your prayer time to increase its meaningfulness.

✠ *Spiritual continuity.* The Stabilizer has a built-in appreciation for tradition, roots, and heritage, a quality which can become a helpful path toward spiritual nurture. I met one person who researched her spiritual family tree, tracing back several generations to people who had spiritual influence on those who had led her to Christ and helped her to grow. Others have been strengthened by writing a spiritual autobiography or a history of their congregation. I have met two persons who spent hours meticulously constructing a replica of the church of their childhood days. Others make pilgrimages to places important in their spiritual journey, taking pictures and bringing back memorabilia to serve as constant reminders of their roots. You can add other ideas to this list. The important point is that while such actions might not fit a traditional view of devotional practices, they may be an especially valuable means of grace to those whose personality type inclines them in these directions.

✠ *Intuitive play.* Earlier in this chapter we noted that since Stabilizers often repress intuition, this function tends to operate immaturely in them and to pop up on its own accord with a negative and foreboding quality. It is important for this personality type to learn to play with intuition in order to allow this side of life to develop and to assume its rightful place as a member of the inner family of mental functions. This may eventually result in enabling the intuitive side to become a valuable source for personal enrichment.

Many find the arts to be a helpful means of exercising the intuitive side. For example, a person studying great poetry and playing with its rich images can explore hitherto hidden dimensions of meaning, and thereby experience the fuller impact of the work. Robert Frost's poetry is sensually beautiful. He is often called a "nature poet," but beneath his descriptions of scenes or events are profound levels of meaning. The attempt to discover some of those levels is one way of playfully exercising the intuitive faculty.

Raising the details of life to higher levels of meaning in order to gain a more global view of the particulars is another function of intuition. By making conscious the larger purposes, ideals, and meanings which motivate our actions, we are playfully engaging this faculty. For example, if you are beginning an exercise program, you might apply different lenses to see that activity in its wider context of meaning. Raised to the first level, perhaps you hope the activity will help you lose weight. The second level is that it will help you fit into last year's wardrobe. Perhaps the third level is that by exercising you will have more energy for your work. While the fourth level helps you remember that by exercising you are giving evidence of your belief that health is an important value in life. When you raise your activity to the fifth level you may be acknowledging that your exercising is a means of being a good steward of God's gifts, and so on. By bringing these different levels to your awareness and articulating them, you are moving out of the purely sensuous mode of perception and are dipping into the intuitive realm.

The Stabilizer's Path toward Wholeness

✠ *Affirm your gifts.* Because you are rather matter-of-fact, you may take for granted the things which you know that you can do, and believe that you are rather objective about the things which you cannot do. However, you may be selling yourself short and underestimating your abilities. Your more notable achievements may have happened because someone else affirmed and valued your abilities and opened up a door which you might not have chosen for yourself.[8] For this reason, it is important for you to spend time considering how your creation gifts are manifested in your life. Thank God daily for these capacities and rededicate them for the fulfillment of His purposes for you.

Because of your inner reserve, you may not often show

others the lighter side of your life—the unexpected associations and often humorous reactions to things going on around you, which you are experiencing inwardly. Others may only see the businesslike you with its stolid exterior. You may be surprised to see how warmly others respond to your other side, and to learn that a more full sharing of your personality will not undermine your reputation of solid dependability. In fact, as you express this side of yourself, your relationships will be enhanced and your other contributions more freely accepted and understood as well.

✠ *Deny your self-will.* You may be predisposed to use your judging capacity on others, sizing up their ideas and coming to rather quick conclusions about their value, accuracy, or relevance. Such judgment could reflect your underlying assumption that your perception is the "right" one. You may discover the Lord challenging you to use your critical faculties to assess your *own* views, as He puts you in situations where He is stretching you to be more tentative about your own conclusions and more open and receptive to the perceptions of others.

Because of your preference for methodical ways of doing things, you may find yourself in contexts where you are having to lay aside your system and practice flexibility. This often happens in family situations when the needs of others combine with the unpredictable nature of living together to turn your personal agenda upside down! Frustration and the attempt to protect your own interests are natural responses. All the while the Lord may be pressing you to deny your self-will; He wants you to know that your worth as a person, your acceptance, your security, and the real source of your effectiveness in life lie in Him and not in some self-imposed regimen, no matter how helpful it has been in the past. Through your willingness to respond in a more relaxed, open, and accepting manner, you may enjoy growth in the grace which "does not seek its own, is not provoked . . . bears all things . . . endures all things."

Sufficient Resources

You give them something to eat. . . . How many loaves do you have?
Mark 6:37-38

———————————————————————

What everyday situations come to your mind when you hear the words *insufficient resources?* Read Mark 6:30-44 aloud.

Remember times past when Christ seemed to multiply your resources and make you sufficient to meet some demanding situation. As you sit quietly in His presence, sense your adequacy in Him.

List all the steps which Christ took in order to meet the crowd's hunger and His disciples' needs. Write down the principles which emerge.

Write two letters, one to Christ regarding some current need in your life and your feelings about it; write the other letter to yourself, expressing what Christ seems to be saying to you now.

Chapter Five

The Crusaders
ENFP and ENTP

Extroverted intuitives are hard to describe because of their infinite variety. Their interest, enthusiasm, and energy pour suddenly into unforeseeable channels like a flash flood, sweeping everything along, overwhelming all obstacles, carving out a path which others will follow long after the force that made it has flowed on into other things.[1]

Case Study: Joshua

Joshua colorfully exemplifies some of the characteristics associated with the Crusaders. Our introduction to Joshua is before Israel's first battle after escaping Egypt. "Moses said to Joshua, 'Choose us some men and go out, fight with Amalek' " (Exodus 17:9). Notice that the first responsibility given to Joshua was not to fight, but to evaluate people. He was to handpick a commando unit to protect the Israelites from an impending Amalekite raid. It was to be a crucial encounter, for not only was the security of the little nomadic nation at stake, but her confidence for the future would depend upon the success of this mission. Moses turned to a young man he knew to have trustworthy intuitive insights into people. Moses had confidence in Joshua's ability to select his comrades wisely.

Later, when Moses had brought the Israelites to the borders of Canaan, the Promised Land, he sent one representative from each of the twelve tribes on a spy mission to reconnoiter the territory, assess the strength of the enemy forces, and evaluate the natural resources of the land. Joshua went along representing the tribe of Ephraim. Upon their return the men reported their findings. Ten of the twelve went beyond the facts, giving a bleak interpretation. Comparing Israel's forces to what appeared to be the enemy's vastly superior strength, they likened themselves to grasshoppers going up against giants!

Joshua and Caleb saw the situation differently. When it came to interpretation, they voted to include *all* of the facts. Why not see the situation in the light of the mighty spiritual resources of the Lord who had miraculously brought them out of Egypt? Why not view the "seen" against the backdrop of the "unseen"? Why not take in the *whole* picture? Joshua was optimistic about their possibilities because he, like Caleb, trusted in more than what his five senses reported. He was convinced in the reality of the invisible world as well. Because of such insight, he could join with Caleb in saying, "We are well able to overcome!" (Numbers 13:30)

Forty years later, after long wandering in the wilderness, the little nomadic nation once again arrived at the shores of the Jordan River. Just prior to crossing and beginning the campaign to "liberate" the land and enter into their promised inheritance, Joshua was appointed as Israel's new leader. As we walk through the chapters of the Bible book which bears his name, we are struck by the qualities which he brought to his role.

✠ *Creativity.* The battle to take Jericho, a masterpiece of strategy, displays Joshua's incredible ingenuity and creativity. Read again the description of the second battle of Ai and the cunning with which he drew the more numerous enemy forces into an ambush. With a map in front of you, trace Canaan's conquest. Notice how, by defeating Jericho and Ai, Joshua managed to open up the interior of Canaan. Observe his use of surprise attack and careful troop deployment, driving a wedge between the southern and northern sections of the country, taking each confederacy in turn. All of this shows the innovative and imaginative gifts of Joshua as he tackled apparently insurmountable obstacles under God's direction.

✠ *Symbolic expression.* Not only are his gifts evidenced by his battle strategies, they are also obvious in the way he worked with his people. After the initial crossing into Canaan at Gilgal, he gathered up the spiritual significance of the place and the moment by leading the nation in a renewal of their covenant with God, with the circumcision of each male as a covenant sign. Then he had a stone memorial erected on the site, using rocks taken from the riverbed over which God had miraculously led them. Finally, Joshua rehearsed with his people the meaning of these symbols, helping them learn how to teach their children in subsequent years when they would ask, "What do these stones mean?" The place, with its signs and symbols, was formative in shaping the spiritual identity of the young nation.

In later years, when Joshua saw his people's need for spiritual refreshment, for reconnecting with their past, and remembering God's purposes for them, he brought them back to Gilgal, their "retreat center." He knew the power of symbolic actions, words, and places for the spiritual journey.

✠ *Vision.* Another characteristic of Joshua's work among his people has to do with vision. He was able to sustain his own perspective and to keep before his people the big picture. Throughout the book there is the recurrence of the Lord's heartening promise, "Be strong and of good courage; do not be afraid, nor be dismayed, for the Lord your God is with you wherever you go" (Joshua 1:9). It runs like a motif through Joshua's life. This promise must have been the focus of his meditation on the eve of many a battle. Joshua had to maintain his perspective of faith lest, in the seemingly endless experience of war, he might grow weary and lose heart. And, as a leader, he served his people by reminding them of this larger frame of reference as well. For example, after the second battle of Ai, he gathered the people all together and read to them all the writings of Moses. He wanted them to see this battle in the context of the great movement of God's plan.

✠ *Insufficient attention to detail.* But the story of Joshua shows some of his weaknesses as well. After Jericho he was riding high and headed for Ai. But his first battle for that city was a humiliating disaster. Why? He went in unprepared. He hadn't gathered sufficient information. He hadn't spent enough time planning his strategy. Apparently he was leaning too much on his ability to be ingenious in the moment of crisis. There he also learned that vitality is drained when sin is harbored in the camp. He apparently never forgot the lessons of Ai.

✠ *Blind trust in intuition.* Joshua's boundless optimism got him into trouble on at least one memorable occasion. By blindly trusting in his own intuition, Joshua made a grave mistake and allowed the Gibeonites to bluff their way into a treaty with him. The writer makes this simple observation, "They did not ask counsel of the Lord" (9:14). Joshua had to learn that his intuition was not an infallible guide, and needed to be subservient to the Lord's direction.

✠ *Attraction to challenge.* The final scene of Joshua's life is particularly revealing. He was a very old man now, giving his farewell address to his nation. He called them to remember God's faithfulness which had brought them to this place of peace. Now what? Sit back and enjoy the land? Protect their investments? No! There were even greater conquests ahead — this time for the citadels of the heart. So Joshua, forever a Crusader, challenges them to start afresh and once again, "Choose for yourselves this day whom you will serve."

Now that we have explored some of the characteristics of this type of personality, illustrated by the life of Joshua, let's isolate some of the Crusader's creation gifts.

The Crusader's Creation Gifts

Of the many traits which could be isolated, we will deal with only four sets here. Keep in mind that some of these characteristics are shared by those who are more introvertive intuitives (the Renewers), but with some interesting contrasts as we shall see in the next chapter.

✠ *Ingenuity and optimism.* A Crusader looks at an "impossible" situation and, rather than feeling despair, is intrigued by it. The wheels begin to turn and the search is on for a way around, over, under, or through the obstacle. Such challenges simply provide the fuel for their engines. If there ceases to be a challenge, the engine loses power, sputters, and falters. It is probably no accident that the Lord, when appointing a leader to take Israel through one battle after another against all odds, chose a person who seemed to exhibit such qualities. For Crusaders, any challenge seems to simply provide an opportunity for the release of their imaginative and innovative abilities to find a solution, with never a thought that the problem could be unsolvable!

One such woman who, in the space of a few days of breaking her ankle, received news that the family auto had been wrecked, her husband's job had been terminated, and that a huge and unexpected bill had arrived, responded, "Whenever the Lord closes a door, He always opens a window! We'll find a way!" To which her husband (probably *not* a Crusader type!) responded, "Honey, if the Lord closes one more door, I'm going to jump out of the nearest window!" For her, the insurmountable odds merely provided a challenge to her sanctified ingenuity.

Their solutions often *are* ingenious. One night I sat in a meeting where we were looking at various options available for the renovation of the athletic facilities of our high school. The main focus was on the football field and the surrounding area. How could we develop more practice areas in order to save the turf on the good field? Each of us was studying the map, trying to envision how to make use of the land adjacent to the playing field. Then, quite suddenly, a Crusader simply turned his map sideways and said, "Why don't we move the bleachers back and turn the football field from east to west, to north and south? That way we can put two fields in the area, even with the addition of new sideline stands." It was a typical flash of ingenuity.

Because of their love for finding solutions to challenging problems, there is a basic optimism in the Crusader. It must have been one of them who remarked, "Impossible simply means that the job might take a little longer, that's all!"

✠ *Inspiration and optimism.* If challenges comprise the fuel which keeps Crusaders going, the fuel is ignited by the fire of inspiration. They simply must see a larger purpose for which they are working. They cannot find joy by simply doing a job; they must be on a *mission!* When they have things in a larger, meaningful perspective, nothing can stop them. However, when their vision fades, so does their energy level![2]

A Crusader friend of mine has a middle-management position which involves planning and administrating in-service training events for staff. If you were to ask him what he does, he would not describe his work in terms of his tasks (planning, coordinating, record-keeping), but he would probably tell you, "I am involved in a program for professional enrichment." His answer would sound more like a mission statement than a job description.

Because Crusaders work by inspiration and because of their great capacity for optimism, they can often be very inspiring to others as well. Like Joshua, they can keep others aware of their larger spiritual purpose, even in the midst of "life in the trenches." However, as may be becoming obvious, there are some types, the Stabilizers, for example, who are rather unmoved by such optimism and inspiration. In fact, they may be rather terrified by launching into the unknown with only inspiration moving the group. They are apprehensive when difficult problems are going to be met by untried and unfamiliar procedures, no matter how creative they may be! They are suspicious when a vision, rather than hard facts, becomes the basis for decisions. When Crusaders run into the resistance which such persons raise, they may tend too quickly to label as the enemy persons who simply require different approaches and who bring different gifts.

✠ *Creativity and originality.* Crusaders are especially open to their intuitions. They live their outer life on the basis of the flow of impressions, hunches, inspirations, flashes of insight, bursts of creativity, imaginative leaps, and breakthrough discoveries. Such material washes up on the shores of awareness from the regions of the unconscious. Intuitive persons prefer to pay attention to this material; they tend to trust what bubbles up to the surface seemingly out of nowhere more than they enjoy focusing on or trusting what they observe with their five senses. As a result, their minds seem to work in almost random fashion, in what Myers called a ski-jump manner.[3] Their minds take off from the known and observed, gathering all sorts of other impressions, relating to myriads of memories, and then swooping back down to land on a point or idea. The difficulty is that intuitive persons would find it difficult to tell another person the intervening steps and how a certain idea came to them, or what really shaped their final decision. And when the idea comes, the decision is focused, the insight breaks through—it arrives with energy and force. It seems to come "from beyond," arriving more as a conviction than just a thought, at times carrying with it even a feeling of destiny. Such an inner certainty can make Crusaders powerfully persuasive . . . and mighty stubborn!

Mildred sat in my office sharing the idea which had literally awakened her from sleep the night before. She got up and went to the kitchen to write down her thoughts, and was so excited that she just stayed up the rest of the night. She couldn't wait to tell me about it. Mildred was president of the woman's organization in our church, a traditional and predictable group which had always used the same basic format for each meeting and generally the same calendar of events, year after year. It had always been that way. No one could remember anything different. But Mildred felt that the group was in a rut. She said, "We are always either thinking just about ourselves, or about some distant land—but hardly ever do we look at the needs here in our own neighborhood, right under our noses!" She then shared her brainstorm. The group could be divided into smaller units, with a monthly competition between the small groups based on reach-out types of projects in the community. Then, the monthly meetings would include reports of those ministry experiments and celebrations together.

I didn't know whether to encourage her or to warn her; I think I remember doing some of both. For the next couple of months I saw the full force of Mildred's personality unleashed on individuals and groups. She was dealing with skepticism, trying to break the power of inertia, and struggling to interpret her dream to a totally mystified woman's society. She never gave up. The group finally bought the idea, and the result was absolutely astounding. I would have never guessed that so much good could have been accomplished by so few people. The entire congregation began to be caught up in the enthusiasm and swept along by the momentum of the women. Our tiny church, which had not had a very high self-image, began to realize how much needed to be done and to discover how much it could do. Its reputation began to spread. Mildred, the Crusader, had brought her gift to us and the blessing spilled over the whole community!

✠ *Insight and perceptivity.* I will touch only briefly on this final set of gifts since the Crusaders share these with the Renewers (chap. 6). But Crusaders often experience a sharp perception into the attitudes and abilities of other people—remember Joshua's first assignment? They will often display an ability to evoke others' gifts and they find a great deal of personal satisfaction in helping other people to develop their capacities.

As parents, Crusaders will probably evidence the ability to envision and encourage each child's possibilities, and delight in finding ways of fostering growth and development.

The Crusader's Infirmities

Of the many areas of potential difficulty, I will highlight three where Crusaders are likely to experience vulnerability.

✠ *Focusing their energies.* Their supply of ideas seems endless. Numerous challenges seem to beckon. They may feel that they are at the mercy of the constantly changing breezes of inspiration. For these reasons, Crusaders may find it difficult to select their targets wisely. They are tempted to spread themselves too thinly and be constantly moving on to the next challenge, before the previous one has been thoroughly addressed. This results in a dissipation of inner power and a subsequent loss of effectiveness.[4] In anticipation of such a tendency, Crusaders do well to make good use of spiritual friends who can help them choose only such projects as would have the highest benefit and return.

One popular writer and preacher receives scores of speaking invitations yearly. He knows that his effectiveness is lost if he takes on too many commitments. He deals with it in two ways. First, he notifies the group which has invited him that decisions about those matters are made on a certain date each year. Second, he utilizes a small team of advisers who pray with him and help him sift through the choices, selecting only those to which they have been guided. Admittedly, not many Crusaders have a problem of this extent, but they may have their own version of it. The use of a small group of special prayer partners, rather than reliance on personal hunches, can be an invaluable resource for helping to focus personal energies on the most productive projects.

✠ *Submitting to group discernment.* Earlier I mentioned that since their inspirations and creative insights often seem to come upon them with such bursts of energy, Crusaders may become amazingly stubborn and singleminded. It is as if they have been swept up by a divine revelation. Such an inner certainty can be a gift, keeping one on course through stormy days and trying times, and leading to singular accomplishments of great good. But this same quality can cause one to foolishly assume that some personal insight is infallible or some project design is above refinement, as if their ideas have divine sanction, if not heavenly origin. Such an attitude can only be described as spiritual arrogance. This unhealthy independence runs counter to the New Testament teaching about mutual ministry and accountability in the body of Christ. In fact, the discipline of submitting to the prayerful discernment and collective wisdom of the group is essential for growth into spiritual maturity.

✠ *Maintaining consistency and faithfulness.* Because of their need for inspiration and for fresh challenges to keep them going, Crusaders may find that follow-through and faithfulness are sometimes problematic. They may seem to drift from one thing to another in a kind of perpetual unrest and endless search, never seeing many things through to completion. How can they deal with such an infirmity? Let's turn now to the nurture of faith in the lives of Crusaders.

Natural Ways for Crusaders to Nourish Faith

✠ *Vow of stability.* In certain monastic orders the brothers take what they call a vow of stability. It is a personal commitment to remain in their particular community through thick and thin, in good times and bad. They refuse a consumer approach to their vocation which would cause them to move to some new place whenever things got a bit boring, the people tiresome, or when something more appealing appeared on the horizon. Crusaders could also benefit from this example and make their own "vow of stability." Upon agreeing to take on a certain job, they might make a spiritual commitment to see the project through to completion. Such an initial dedication could enable them to find staying power on those days when things seemed to drag and inspiration wanes. Such an act might be a spiritual discipline of great importance, fostering the growth of that special fruit of the spirit which is called faithfulness.

✠ *Prayer of silence.* Crusaders are especially oriented toward the future and its possibilities. They are drawn to those situations which call forth their creativity and ingenuity. It is important that this creation gift be offered up to the Lord. One way that this can be done is through the prayer of silence, as one waits upon God. Remember Joshua's lesson when he had depended overmuch on his own intuitions and took premature action? Scripture notes that he did not "ask counsel of the Lord." By waiting on God in silence, one consciously slows down the rush to action and deliberately seeks divine counsel. Such periods of prayerful silence are essential in order for the intuitive person to become attentive to those images and inspirations through which the Lord often chooses to communicate Himself.

In the last few years I have been privileged to get to know the Korean minister, Dr. Sundo Kim, who pastors the world's largest Methodist church, located in Seoul. On one evening as I was visiting with him he asked if I would like to see his power room. He went to one end of his study and opened a closet door. From the ceiling of the little room there hung a light bulb. On one wall was a picture of Jesus. On the floor was a small cushion. It was his special prayer place. "I do not go home on Saturday nights, but spend them here in my study preparing for Sunday morning. I study and write for a while at my desk; then, when I am stuck and need an illustration or am searching for a way to give shape to some idea, I will move to my power room and simply tell Jesus my need and wait silently for Him, until the thoughts begin to flow again. Then I move back to my desk and write some more." Such a silent waiting is an important, but sometimes forgotten, way of nurturing the life of faith.

It is also important to share with others the inspirations which come through this prayerful seeking. In this way the idea can be tested, so that the Crusaders can avoid the temptation of identifying their own thoughts with divine revelation, or living independently of the body of Christ.

✠ *The power of the symbolic.* On the eve of the first battle, Joshua must have been flooded with many uncertainties and doubts. It can even happen to a Crusader! "And it came to pass, when Joshua was by Jericho, that he lifted his eyes and looked, and behold, a Man stood opposite him with His sword drawn in His hand" (Joshua 5:13).

The ensuing conversation is highly symbolic and loaded with power for Joshua. He asked the stranger, "Are You for us or for our adversaries?" To which came the reply, "No, but as Commander of the army of the Lord I have now come." This divine representative was saying that He was not an ally, but that He was to be the *real* Leader in the battles ahead. The meaning of this strange encounter was profound. Whatever gifts Joshua happened to possess, it was not *he* who was expected to bear the full weight of responsibility. He was simply a servant who was to make himself available for the Lord's purposes. "And Joshua fell on his face to the earth and worshiped, and said to Him, 'What does my Lord say to His servant?' " (5:14)

The symbolic will often have rich importance in nurturing the faith of Crusaders. It is not unusual for them to find that an event, a word, a scene, or a dream becomes a kind of window into eternity. It takes on for them the spiritual significance of a parable, loaded with meaning which they will continue to ponder for instruction and inspiration, sometimes for years.

The Crusader's Path toward Wholeness

✠ *Affirm your gifts.* The story of Joshua's Visitor leads us to the important issue of growth in the life of Crusaders. As they affirm their gifts, they will need to remain conscious of the "not I but Christ" principle. Joshua had to recognize that, whatever his abilities, he had to allow the Lord to lead the battles. He had to discover that his own intuitions could not be identified directly with the voice of God. He had to learn the supple humility of living as a servant of the Lord.

In a diary entry in 1867, Hannah Whithall Smith put it so well:

> Whether in temptation or in service, if we cease from our own plan and our own activities, leaving the care and ordering of our work to Him, He will plan for us, work through us, and use us as His instruments to accomplish His own purposes of love and mercy. The responsibility will be all His; we need only be obedient.... Everywhere and in everything we are nothing and Christ is all.[5]

✠ *Deny your self-will.* As you offer yourself to the Lord, you may find that He sometimes places you in situations where, rather than having the freedom to scout out new possibilities and respond to fresh challenges, you are having to work with the myriads of details involved in the implementation of some plan, or you are having to attend to the routine and repetitive aspects of the daily grind. You may be tempted to become "weary in well-doing" and to allow your restlessness to breed in you a spirit of resentment.

Whenever such occasions arise, prayer becomes essential. You will need to focus on the highest level of purpose of all. "*Whatever* you do, do *all* for the glory of God"—even the things which seem so boring and irksome! In such times you will need to reach out to the body of Christ around you to find refreshment through the ministries of others. You will learn to consult with and seek assistance from those who have special gifts for doing the things which are most difficult for you. Such self-offering may become a significant occasion for growth in God's grace. You, who might have preferred to move on to some other opportunity or to daydream about some future challenges, will be discovering the profound spiritual lesson of loving acceptance of all that God sends you to do in each moment. In his classic *The Joy of Full Surrender*, Jean de Caussade wrote of this experience, saying that such a loving acceptance "consists of accepting what most frequently cannot be avoided, and in bearing with love, consolation, and sweetness, that which we too often endure with weariness and irritation."[6]

Who Leads?

> *What does my Lord say to His servant?*
> Joshua 5:14

———————————————————

You are Joshua on the eve of your first campaign, with the responsibility of leading your tiny nation into battle against enormous odds. You've gone out to be alone. What are you feeling? What are you needing? Read Joshua 5:13-15 in a soft voice.

Ponder the image of the mysterious Visitor. Who is He? How have you met Him yourself? What is the inner meaning of the answers He gives to Joshua's questions?

Study a commentary on this passage. Make notes about the meaning and significance of this episode for Joshua. Write down the spiritual principle for your own life.

Realize that you are in the Lord's presence. Pray with your body as Joshua did (lie on the floor, take off your shoes). Pour out your heart to Him about the most difficult situation you face.

Chapter Six

The Renewers
INFJ and INTJ

Renewers are the rarest of all the personality types and their unique gifts enrich our lives in many ways. They are creative persons whose ideas and insights are often instrumental in producing innovative change in our organizations, giving fresh perspectives on our situations, and enabling our latent personal gifts to emerge.

Case Study: John

The Gospel of John illustrates some of the qualities of the introvertive intuitive person. This is not the place to enter into a debate as to how this Gospel was produced. Suffice it to say that there is a close connection between John the Apostle and this book, whether he dictated it, supplied another with the bulk of the material for it, or was actually the one who put the pen to paper and produced it. Regardless, the power of his personality, the closeness of his relationship with Christ, and the depth of his understanding of our Lord shine through on every page.

John the Beloved was the younger of Zebedee's sons. He and his brother James both became Jesus' followers. If their mother was Salome (as Mark 16:1 and Matthew 27:56 may indicate), it means that John was a cousin to Jesus on his mother's side, since Salome was Mary's sister.

The bare facts of his life show that he left a prosperous

fishing business in order to join Jesus' band. He and his brother earned the nickname, Sons of Thunder, because of their sometimes hotheaded reactions to situations and people. John helped to arrange the details for the Last Supper. He was the only one of Jesus' disciples to stay by the cross during the Crucifixion; the others seemed to have fled to save their own skins. It was to John that the dying Jesus entrusted the care of His mother, Mary.

It was John who ran to the empty tomb and pondered the meaning of the undisturbed graveclothes lying where Jesus' body had been laid. He was the first of the fishermen to recognize that the mysterious figure on the shore of Tiberius was actually Jesus, alive from the dead. John established the first Christian church in Jerusalem and was instrumental in the forming of Christian congregations in Ephesus and Asia Minor.

In the Gospel which bears his name, we get our clearest picture of the personality of this disciple whom Jesus loved. The material which he brought, the profundity of his reflection, the way he organized and presented it, all bear the Renewer's stamp.

✠ *Depth.* Notice John's depth. While the other Gospel writers presented the facts about Jesus' life and death, John wanted to display the rich meanings of those facts. His Gospel is more like a great mural than an album of photographs. Where the other writers provide us with their own structuring and sequencing of stories and quotations from Jesus, John's account allows Jesus to be more expressive, filling out the underlying meanings of His teachings. For example, in this Gospel Jesus doesn't simply say, "I am the vine, you are the branches." John lets Jesus show how our lives are fed by Him and tended by the Father to produce various harvests of fruit appropriate to the extent of our adherence to Him. In His encounter with Nicodemus, Jesus didn't just say, "You must be born again." He elaborated about the Spirit's mysterious power, His own spiritual authority, the necessity that He be lifted up, and the wonder of God's love. As the discourse continues, it is difficult to know whether it is still Jesus speaking to Nicodemus or John speaking to us. As a Renewer, John interacted with and reflected deeply upon the words of Christ.

In his Gospel, he not only brings us the glory of the facts, but also the richness of his insights.

✠ *Artistry.* John is also more artistic and creative than the other Gospel writers in the way he presents his material. For example, look at his depiction of Jesus' arguments in debate. Rather than moving from premise to conclusion, John presents Jesus' arguments as insights into the truth, treating truth as if it were a perfect crystal which could be turned in an endless variety of ways to reveal its various facets and to catch its infinite combinations of color. William Temple called such an approach more artistic than scientific, and spoke of how much better it fitted John's material, since he was presenting a truth which was not dependent on or derivative of some other truth, but which stood alone and needed to make its own impact upon the mind and heart.[1]

✠ *Symbol.* John shows the Renewer's fascination with symbol, sign, and image. For example, John is the Gospel writer who records Jesus' play with words and their various levels of meaning. Temple (2:19-21), birth (3:3-4), water (4:14-15), and food (4:32-33) all have a deeper meaning than their hearers first recognized. A superficial interpretation left them bewildered. Spiritual understanding required the exercise of imagination. John loved Jesus' imagery as He spoke of Himself as a door, shepherd, light, bread, etc. Each image became a portal through which we could glimpse another aspect of His true nature. John also recorded seven events in Jesus' life as signs, for in them faith recognized eternity breaking into time.

✠ *Future/present.* Finally, John's Gospel is eschatological. It anticipates end times and Jesus' second coming. But John telescopes these final things in such a way that he always sees the present in the light of the future (the whole Gospel is written from a Resurrection perspective) and he presents the future as already operative in the here and now. For example, while certain that Christ will come again in the future, John recognizes that in a real sense He has already come again through the giving of His Spirit. While pointing toward a future fulfillment to the promise of eternal life, he also recognizes that this life can be appropriated *now*. While assuring us of a coming judgment, John is also just as certain that in Christ this judgment has already come upon us. In the pages ahead, we will see how it is always characteristic for a Renewer to see the present in terms of the future, and how Renewers often help us to experience the power of the "not yet" in the "here and now."

The Renewer's Creation Gifts

There are three essential sets of gifts which the Renewers bring to us—their insight and vision, their inspiration and motivation, and their reminders to us of possibility and potentiality.

✠ *Insight and vision.* As introvertive persons, Renewers work privately with their intuitive insights, pondering their meanings and implications, sounding their depths and exploring their richness before they share them with others. We certainly see this in John's life. In fact, one may know a Renewer for a long time before ever being allowed into this inner sanctuary. Then, when you are finally invited inside, you discover what was motivating your friend all along, and you realize how little you really understood about this person. Because of their sense of privacy, they tend to be reluctant to share their deepest insights. So, in groups, for example, you may find that Renewers may be rather quiet, but when they do speak it is usually worth the wait! They often possess the ability to communicate with eloquence, typically in the language of symbol and imagery.

Those who are INTJs (with Thinking as their auxiliary function) are typically *revitalizers of things*. They develop what amounts to a mental picture of what could be, and then relate their vision to others, working with them to bring it into existence. An INTJ friend of mine is such a revitalizer. When he takes a new position, faces a fresh challenge, or is given a new responsibility, his very first move is usually to size up the situation, looking at what has been done in the past to see how things may be turned around in a novel fashion, in order to make them work better and more efficiently.

On the other hand, INFJ Renewers (who have Feeling as an auxiliary) often express their gifts through *revitalizing people*. Another friend of mine, when taking on a new position or being given a new opportunity, typically focuses on the persons involved. He gathers impressions and considers how persons might be released in more fulfilling ways, and then tries to translate his vision into reality through whatever channels are available.

Whether by reorganizing things or renewing persons, Renewers make their contribution by initiating change based on their unique perceptions of our situations. You will have noticed that the Renewers trust deeply in their own private assessment which is arrived at intuitively. Intuition is a valid and important gift. It is important that Renewers learn to attend to and trust these personal insights. Such inner work is quite naturally characterized by independence. But an intuitive grasp of a situation does not automatically imply an awareness and assessment of all the facts, since facts require attention to sensory data, and it is hard to pay attention to two things at once! For this reason, Renewers need to resist their (occasional) natural tendency toward stubbornness and listen to the observations and criticisms of others! Otherwise their gift may actually turn into an infirmity!

One intuitive, married to a sensing person, was helping his wife prepare for company. She probably should have known better, but she asked him to read her the recipe aloud as she collected the ingredients for the pumpkin pie. It called for one pound of pumpkin. She puzzled as to whether the can he held in his hand was a pound (its weight wasn't printed on the label). He announced confidently — "Yes, this is a pound. Says so right here on the label — 'one can equals one pound.' " When the pie was taken out of the oven a little later, it bore no resemblance to her intentions. She picked up the can and this time read the label for herself (alas, too late!). "One can equals one *cup*." Evidently her husband had grasped intuitively the words on the label, rather than getting an accurate report from his senses!

✠ *Inspiration and motivation.* "A person who has a *why* to live can bear almost any *how*." I don't know whether Nietzsche was a Renewer in our sense of the word, but his famous dictum certainly applies to the Renewers. These persons need a compelling purpose and a sense of meaning to enable them to function well in life. "It's your job" or "Do it because you *have* to" are simply unsatisfying motivators for them. Mother Teresa of Calcutta understood this when she said to a discouraged nun who wanted to abandon her exhausting work with dying persons, "Next time, see the one with whom you are working as the Lord Himself. What you do for the beggar, do it for Jesus." She realized the absolute necessity for this type of person to raise the immediate task to a higher level of meaning. Only in this way could the inner fire be kept burning in a dark and dismal situation.

✠ *Possibility and potentiality.* John's way of living the present in the light of the future, and of experiencing the power of the "not yet" in the "here and now," certainly applies to the Renewers. Today's assignments awaken dreams of tomorrow's possibilities. Standard procedures whet their appetites for innovative approaches. What others may view as problems become their challenges. Their intuition tells them that any mountain can be moved and their imagination enables them to picture the contours of this new landscape while others are still adjusting to detour signs!

The Renewer's Infirmities

✠ *Loneliness.* It is estimated that 75 percent of the population of the United States prefers extroversion over introversion, and that 75 percent also prefer sensing over intuition.[2] This implies that of all the types, the introvertive intuitives are in the minority. They will probably spend more energy trying to understand and be understood than any of the other groups. The weight will fall on them to come out of themselves in order to meet others more than halfway. When this observation is coupled with the realization that the Renewers are also the most independent of all the personality types, we can begin to understand why these persons may sometimes experience intense personal loneliness. It can happen even if they are happily married, respected by their colleagues, and surrounded by people. Of all the personality groups, they will need to learn to make the spiritual passage from loneliness to solitude. And rather than withdraw from others when personally hurt or discouraged, they will need to practice turning deliberately toward the community of faith.

✠ *Restlessness.* Restlessness is another infirmity borne by many Renewers. They can become bogged down by the mundane and ordinary. They crave fresh challenges and opportunities. They may become so absorbed with their thoughts and insights that they miss much that the present moment brings. Awareness of and strategies for dealing with this tendency are important for the Renewer parent. Otherwise, one may live half a step removed from the glorious little events of daily life.

Sometimes Renewers speak of having a destiny which they must discover and fulfill, as if it were an elusive mystery. Of course, we all do have a destiny! We are to bring honor to God by living out Christful lives through His strength in the midst of our present circumstances. But it is possible for our romantic notions about destiny to cause us to miss the very purpose for our existence.

A Renewer had a dream one night. In his dream he met a beggar who promised him that if he would surrender all of his possessions he would give him a key which would unlock a vast treasure. The man accepted the offer and, handing over all that he owned, received the key, was pointed toward an underground passage and told, "Enter and follow the path to the treasure." He began his journey but shortly came up against a huge, immovable, rock door. He strained and pushed but it would not budge. He was almost ready to give up when he remembered his key. By inserting it into the lock, the huge door swung open freely and he was on his way again. A little later he had the same experience, this time coming to a cast-iron door. Once again he struggled and pushed but to no avail. Then, remembering his key, he was able to gain entry into the next section. This experience was repeated many times until, just ahead, he could see daylight. Soon he would be back to ground level. His heart ached because he realized that he had given up everything for nothing. He turned to take one last look down the long passage through which he had traveled.

Just then he saw something which sparkled and gleamed. He went back a few steps and realized that the back of the door through which he had just come was encrusted with jewels inlaid in gold. Retracing his way he found that the same was true of the back of every door through which he had passed! Then he realized that at every turn he had been meeting the treasure which he sought, but had not realized it! When the Renewer awakened, he pondered the meaning of the dream. He realized that he had been in search of an illusive treasure, but that at every turn in his life's passage he had actually been meeting it. The treasure was simply ordinary things seen in a spiritual light, and the key which unlocked the doors was his faith!

✠ *Indulgence.* Because the most used faculty of the Renewer is intuition, the least used of the four mental functions is sensing. Since the senses are the least used and the least trusted, they represent the most repressed and most immature dimension of the Renewer's life. For this reason, the Renewers (and possibly the Crusaders) will be more susceptible than the other types to temptations to grossly indulge their senses. The repressed side of their lives may pop up from time to time in a childish fashion, demanding attention. Physical appetites may become like the undertow of the surf, powerfully pulling them down. Temptations to eating binges, entertainment gluts, dwelling on sexual fantasies, and the crudest license are just some of the ways in which they might experience their weakness. But infirmity is not sin. While increasing one's vulnerability, it does not inevitably lead to transgression. It is a weakness which can be anticipated and for which the Renewer can learn to prepare. We will return to this idea in the last section of this chapter.

✠ *Overextension.* A final area of special difficulty for Renewers is also related to their giftedness. Because they work by inspiration, they can become so absorbed in a project that they seem to lose track of all else. They are undoubtedly the ones who inspire all the absent-minded professor stories. They tend to hit streaks when they are so engrossed that they forget to eat, lose all track of time, and seem to be driven by boundless energy. They can keep going at this level of intensity longer than you would imagine. It is as if they were intoxicated by what they are doing. Much to their surprise, they are often rudely awakened to their humanity. It may come in the form of flulike symptoms, utter depletion, or a sense of depression. They wonder what they caught, not realizing that it is really a question of what caught them! Because they at times fall prey to overextension and the physical toll which it takes, they will need to find ways of anticipating such situations and being good stewards of their physical health.

Natural Ways for Renewers to Nourish Faith

The use of the imaginative faculties provide the Renewers their most natural path for spiritual nurture. One Renewer spoke of his great relief when he discovered that the difficulties which he experienced in trying to follow a prescribed pattern for his morning devotions were due to personality type and not spiritual inadequacy! He had to find a way which was suited to him, rather than trying to copy someone else. Thomas à Kempis gave such advice in his immortal classic, *The Imitation of Christ*. "Tailor-make your private devotions; some exercises suit certain persons better than others."[3] What are some of the devotional aids which might be particularly helpful to the introvertive intuitives?

✠ *Imaging prayer.* The creative use of imaging can be especially invigorating for Renewers. Of course, the idea of imaging raises a red flag for some, because of the negative critique which has been made of this approach. However, the Lord seems to affirm the validity of the imaginative faculty—else why would there be such an abundance of story, parable, symbol, and imagery in the Gospels? In fact, it was through such means that Jesus sought to engage His hearers and to involve them in His teachings. Of course, we are not encouraging the undisciplined use of imagination. In meditation, one's imagination is always guided by the context of the passage and by the thrust of scriptural teaching on a given subject.

One approach to the use of imagination in meditation is the Ignatian method. I stumbled on it quite accidentally as I was trying to find a way of using the Bible with my small children just before they went to sleep at night. Having had limited success with the Bible storybook, I simply began telling them the Bible stories, but in a special way. I invented two little characters, Joel and Anna, who were about seven or eight years old. I allowed them to be present, in the background, at the various occasions of Jesus' ministry. I attempted to tell the story from their eyes. The interesting thing was that I got caught up in it myself! I found that it helped me when I imagined the scene vividly, as if I were there. I began to discover the remarkable principle that a story which is vividly pictured can be as powerful as an event in which you are actually physically present. I found that such an imaginative involvement with Scripture leads one into engagement with the Living Lord.

Later I read Douglas Steere's *The Dimensions of Prayer* and found out that what I was doing had a name—it is called the Ignatian method of meditation. Both Ignatius' *Spiritual Exercises* and Frances De Sales' readable classic, *Introduction to the Devout Life,* helped me to understand this process better. You may wish to track those sources in order to find out more about this way of praying the Gospels.

✠ *Symbol.* Renewers may also find that symbols help them to enter into a consciousness of the Lord's nearness. Religious art, for example the remarkable character studies in Rembrandt's paintings of biblical scenes, can be an important devotional aid. Likewise an intuitive person can find great meaning in a lit candle, a cross, or even an object from nature such as a stone or a leaf. Julian of Norwich found that holding a hazelnut in her hands, clothes blowing in the wind, or a vision of the seabed were laden with spiritual meanings.[4] The intuitive person finds that art, nature, and life experiences have the power to evoke images which, upon reflection, yield meanings which stir and enrich the inner life.

✠ *Creative writing.* Another devotional aid which is often helpful to intuitive persons is the use of creative writing, either their own or someone else's. Great poetry with all of its images and metaphors can open up spiritual insights. Allegorical writings such as those of George MacDonald and C.S. Lewis are useful in stimulating their imaginative faith. Writing their own poetry, recording their spiritual insights in a journal, doing their own artwork—even doodling—can be ways of opening themselves up to God.

I have told you of my conviction that the intuitive's creative imagination still needs the discipline of Scripture in order for the spiritual life to be formed according to God's design. While all of the ideas above (and many others which will come to your mind) can enrich the Renewer's devotional life, I believe that a consistent discipline of Bible study and Scripture memorization must undergird their growth.

The Renewer's Path toward Wholeness

✠ *Affirm your gifts.* It is important that you learn to affirm your gifts in the midst of a society which sometimes stresses equally valid but quite contrary ways of living. The intuitive insight is a valid source of information and one from which significant wisdom can flow. The fruits of your rich inner life will sometimes be a vital source of inspiration to those around you. The goodness of this gift for the community will depend not only on how much you trust and develop your intuition, but also on how much you are willing to entrust your insights to others.

✠ *Deny your self-will.* You have already noticed that the senses pay the price of your preference for living in the intuitive domain. It will be important for your growth toward wholeness that, more and more, you find ways of affirming your senses and learning to enjoy them. Play can become very important for you in this regard. So can prayer. By practicing some of the ideas offered in the section on Nurture for Energizers, difficult as these may be for you at first, you may experience fresh winds of the Spirit in your own spiritual life.

You will often be tempted to drive yourself past your own limits, to your detriment and to the hurt of others around you. The Lord will call you to disciplined ways of ordering your life which give proper regard to physical needs and your personal relationships.

You will sometimes find that when you are particularly tired or stressed you will experience the undertow of indulgence — sometimes to your great regret afterward. By anticipating such experiences you may find new freedom. For example, the proper care of your body to avoid overextension, the right balance of play and enjoyment in order to allow the Sensing dimension its own place in your life, and dependence on (rather than independence of) the body of Christ in your times of need — all will be important resources for you. Exercising yourself in these directions may not come easily or naturally, but they may be extremely important for your growth in Christ.

Fruit...More Fruit...Much Fruit

> *I am the vine, you are the branches. He who abides in Me, and I in him, bears much fruit; for without Me you can do nothing.*   John 15:5

Read John 15:1-8, with your fingers guiding your eyes across the lines and allowing your touch to linger on particular words. Take time to notice what Christ says to His disciples. Recall the context.

Personalize this passage by inserting your own name after the word *you* each time it occurs. Read the passage slowly and allow Christ to speak it to you.

What are some of the ways in which the Father prunes our lives? What is the fruit of which Christ speaks? How does one abide in Him? Summarize your thoughts by writing them out.

Turn this passage into a prayer. Verse by verse, adapt the words so that they become a confession of your faith, love, and commitment to Christ. "Lord Jesus, You are my vine, the source of my life."

Chapter Seven

The Organizers
ESTJ and ENTJ

Organizers make great contributions to our lives. They bring us their ability to size up things with an eye for how an idea might be developed or problems solved so that our lives might be more effective or efficient. They seem born to lead and may be quite capable at doing so!

Case Study: Solomon

Of the several biblical characters who might represent the Organizers, none stands out quite so vividly to me as Solomon. While much could be written about him, I'll simply highlight the parts of his story which suggest some of the Organizers' distinctive personal traits.

From his boyhood people started becoming aware of Solomon's wisdom. Evidently he could look over a situation and, through logic or insight, know what ought to be done about it. When his father, David, had him anointed as King of Israel, Solomon showed his sagacity (and ruthlessness?) by deporting some of his enemies and executing others in order to solidify his position. Shrewdly he married the daughter of the Pharaoh of Egypt, cementing a treaty with this southern empire in order to establish a better chance for peace in his own country.

When God appeared to Solomon in a dream and asked him to name his heart's desire, Solomon humbly acknowledged his limitations and his great need for an "understanding heart" and for discernment to know good and evil so that he could be a just leader. In other words, he longed for the increase of those very qualities which he had already evidenced and which he prized so highly. He acknowledged that only the Lord could provide him with such wisdom. God answered his prayer and intensified his native capacities.

Solomon loved to make decisions, to lead, and to organize. These traits were demonstrated throughout his career, from the way he organized his government to the creation of a management structure which efficiently supervised a labor force of over 183,000 men when the temple was being built.

As his story unfolds, we observe how Solomon collected friends around him who served as his advisers. This became a dangerous filter, for he was less likely to receive the kind of information which could have deepened his understanding and possibly saved him from some of the tragic mistakes which followed in later years. He lived under the illusion that his lavish lifestyle could (and should) be supported by his kingdom. He built homes and palaces so exquisite that their descriptions tax historians' abilities. His opulence bled his country dry. Becoming intoxicated with his own abilities and with the praise of others, he lost his sense of humility and stewardship before God. His final years were marked by his moral collapse and the disintegration of his great kingdom.

Not a pretty sight! But this case study serves to illustrate some of the valuable traits of the Organizers, while also reminding us of their very human infirmities.

The Organizer's Creation Gifts

Literature is rich with examples of the traits of this group we are calling the Organizers.[1] Here we will draw on six typical qualities which make these persons quickly recognizable.

✠ *Leadership.* One quickly recognizes the Organizer's leadership inclination. If a group of people were snowbound in a public building, the Organizer would likely be the first one to step forward with suggestions of what needed to be done, and be prepared to delegate various responsibilities.

✠ *Structure.* The Organizer has a knack for seeing how things can be structured and planned in efficient and logical ways. From flow charts at work and "to-do" lists in the home, the Organizer needs to bring order out of chaos. Her notebook might be sectioned, separating the compartments of her life, or her kitchen calendar might show her "divide and conquer" approach to the various tasks ahead that day. Being systematic is an important value to the Organizer. Things will almost always be scheduled; punctuality—with meals or appointments—is a virtue to them, while variance with the plan can be a cause of real frustration.

✠ *Goal-orientation.* The Organizer knows where he or she is going. In fact, not to have a plan, not to be working toward some project or following some vision, is almost unthinkable. The Organizer is a "take charge" kind of person, a doer of deeds, and a fulfiller of objectives. For this person you could say in truth, "Work is his life." That makes it hard for the Organizer to take a real vacation, or set aside time to truly relax. One Organizer whom I knew was told that he needed to take some time off to unwind every week. In order to "accomplish this goal"(!) he decided to watch one particular TV program every Thursday night. A few weeks later when I asked him about the progress he was making with his new resolution he told me, "It's going great! I look forward to Thursday evenings. I watch the TV with my legal pad at hand, and take notes on the moral themes which are treated in the script! I'm making a study of the show's moral values." He didn't even crack a smile when he reported this "success"!

The Organizer's impatience with persons who are laid back—seeing them as aimless and lacking in ambition—sometimes makes the Organizer a difficult person under whom to work. But it is important to remember that Organizers are at least as hard on themselves as they are on others around them.

A parent who is an Organizer can experience exasperation and probably create frustration all around, by trying to remold a basically spontaneous and impulsive child into his own image. On the other hand, the Organizer's child will always know what the parent expects and will likely be clear about the consequences of failing to perform to those expectations!

✠ *Decisiveness.* Myers tells of receiving a letter from an Organizer who wrote:

> Say something about the almost irresistible urge to make decisions, just for their own sake. Under this urge I will not only make quick and accurate decisions *in my own field,* but will tend to make equally quick but *faulty* decisions in a strange field, just because I'm intent on decisions and do not take time to perceive the facts fully.[2]

This reminds us of the sad case of Solomon, who lost both perspective and humility. He made bad decisions because he did not have sufficient facts before him. He apparently listened only to those who flattered him. While decisiveness can be a great gift, it must be balanced with perception. Things must be seen in proper perspective, or the Organizer can choose the wrong goals or decide on the wrong course of action.

The humility to be open to uncomfortable information, the commitment to work for the good of the people rather than for enhancing one's own position or possessions, and the discipline of waiting on the Lord are all essential if the Organizer is to become a person of true wisdom.

✠ *Impersonality.* Organizers' gifts lie in being able to see the big picture, to figure out what could be done, and to organize for action. Their "task orientation" may render them rather oblivious to the feelings of others. Of course, this can be a great advantage when the pursuit of a worthy goal meets the kind of opposition which would likely deflate or derail other personality types. Organizers can be remarkably thick-skinned, taking criticism in stride and not being knocked off-balance as they pursue their goals single-mindedly. But while Organizers are finding fulfillment in the job itself or in their quest, they may lose sight of the fact that there are others around them who need to draw strength from affirmation and recognition.

Sometimes people working with the Organizers will end up feeling unheard, used, and treated as things instead of being valued as persons. This may breed in them a sense of discouragement and depression (repressed anger) which affects their own performance. The Organizer may misread these symptoms, interpreting as disloyalty that which is actually a cry for respect.

Of course, this same impersonality can also show up at home. A spouse may feel taken for granted, or a child may feel the need to make an appointment with the "boss" in order to have a little undivided attention. Family members may often feel the pressure of criticism when things are not done perfectly, on schedule, or according to the Organizer's plan; they rarely feel the pleasure of compliments about the things which were done well or when goals (other than those of the Organizer!) were pursued and accomplished.

✠ *Routineness.* A final characteristic, common to many Organizers, is that they may like to live by formulas and routines. Structure and organization, standard operating procedures and schedules, give them a sense of security and confidence. There are many ways in which set patterns can be made to serve the needs of the Organizer.

Formulas can be applied at work in the form of checklists and daily routines. This gives a certain dependable regularity to their work. It reduces complications and assures that things will happen in an orderly and predictable fashion.

Formulas may be applied at home. Schedules may be devised to include times for recreation, socializing with friends, and working on the marital relationship through shared experiences. In such ways, Organizers can take care of some areas which they may be tempted to overlook. "But that lacks spontaneity," someone may protest. However, premeditation may in fact demonstrate a thoughtfulness and consideration which are authentic expressions of love and demonstrations of sincerity. It is better for Organizers to show "intentional care" than to have to submit a relationship to "intensive care" for treatment!

Formulas may be fruitful in their spiritual lives as well. Such an idea may strike another personality type as odd, even dangerous, since it might open the door to meaningless ritualism. However, before judging too harshly, realize that we all seem to be drawn to spiritual patterns which fit us best. We will return to this thought later in this chapter.

The Organizer's Infirmities

What are some areas of vulnerability which the Organizer needs to anticipate? Since there are some similarities with the Analyzers (chap. 8), I will highlight only two distinctive infirmities here.

✠ *Tunnel vision.* Organizers may develop tunnel vision and see only what they want to see. In other words, they may accept only such input as confirms their own analysis of the situation and supports the decision to which they are already committed. Remember Solomon? He seemed to gather his own yes-men around him and did not allow negative input which might have challenged some of his pet projects on the basis of the drain which those operations would put upon the economy. In anticipation of this temptation, perhaps Organizers need to incorporate into their Rule of Life that they will suspend judgment and delay decisions until they have collected and considered information from points of view contrary to their own. They will need to take seriously the concept of the body of Christ, realizing that whatever organizational gifts they may possess, they also need the perceptions and contributions of others in order to act wisely and for the good of all.

✠ *Treating persons as things.* Organizers may tend to be so "task oriented" and "project driven" that they fail to pay sufficient attention to the feelings of others. In anticipation of the temptation to treat persons as things, Organizers may do well to set up reminders to attend to the personal dimension by recognizing others' achievements and affirming their actions.

Probably the most compelling task of all for Organizers will be the practice of unhurried and focused listening. There is no greater way of treating another personally than attentive listening. This includes being receptive to both the feelings and the ideas of another, without judging hastily or interrupting prematurely in order to solve the other's problem.

The practice of intercessory prayer for persons in their family, fellow workers, or church members may become a way in which Organizers may also grow in their capacity to see other persons from God's viewpoint. Such a vision may help them to ease up on the trigger of criticism and impatience, and help them to practice appreciation and understanding.

Natural Ways for Organizers to Nourish Faith

Those who are in the tradition of Solomon will probably nurture their faith in a manner consistent with all else that they do. In chapter 2, we noted that although God can speak directly to one's spirit, He typically uses our most receptive channel to communicate Himself to us. Let's take a closer look at what this may imply for the Organizers. The following suggestions are merely illustrative and by no means exhaust all the possibilities.

✠ *Action and reflection.* The spirituality of Organizers will likely be marked by action. They will probably find it difficult to leave matters in theory. For them, theology must be applied. They will be persons of action and *may* grow spiritually in the very process of organizing for ministry, tackling problems, working out solutions, and striving for results. You will notice that I said that they *may* grow as they engage in such active ministry. Actually such growth will depend on two things which we noted in our case study on Solomon. In his early years, his life was especially blessed because of his capacity to recognize God as the source of his gifts and to realize that he could do nothing apart from the Lord's assistance. Also important was his awareness that he was called to live for the glory of God.

It was when Solomon began to be obsessed with his need to live for his own selfish desires that his life took a dramatically downward turn. A willing surrender of gifts, conscious dependence on God, and dedication to put energies to work for His glory, are all essential qualities for the Organizer to experience spiritual growth through self-investment. This implies that the Organizer's activity needs to be balanced with reflection and prayer. Only by adoration of the Almighty Lord, seeing life (including their activities) in the light of His greatness and glory, can proper perspective be maintained. Otherwise a vessel of God may begin to mistake itself for the source!

✠ *Mental and written prayer.* For Organizers, prayer is the likely occasion to express thoughts to God. Thoughts are organized into words, ideas are carefully translated into language. The mind is fully engaged, giving form to prayer. For that reason, they may find their prayer life enriched by writing out their own prayers and drawing from this personal collection in their daily prayertime. Or they might find it meaningful to use the written prayers of others.

Unfortunately, written prayers are suspect in certain evangelical circles. Some would say, "If you cannot express yourself to God in your own words, but have to rely on the written prayers of others, then you must not have a very vital personal relationship with Christ!" Such a criticism fails to remember that praying with our forefathers in the faith has always been part of the tradition of the church. After all, the Book of Psalms is basically a book of written prayers. The criticism also fails to respect our basic differences in personality. We should not find fault with what another finds helpful in developing a personal relationship with the Lord, unless there is some genuine theological faultline which will lead to heresy.

But since mental activity may be so primary in the Organizer's prayer life, that very effort can sometimes get in the way. A person's attention may be so occupied with thinking and forming thoughts into the right words that simple, quiet receptivity to the gift of God's presence is missed. Stillness, silence, and waiting on the Lord are important avenues for balance and growth in the Organizer's spiritual life.

✠ *Rule of life.* Since the Organizer finds it helpful to adopt standard procedures for dealing with daily activities, this quality can also be brought to bear in the spiritual life. The saints of the ages sometimes used what they called a Rule of Life in which they summarized their goals and aspirations with regard to faithfulness in their life with God. The rule served them in somewhat the same fashion as the checklist in the cockpit of an airplane. Before every flight the copilot reads the list, item by item, while the pilot makes sure that all essentials have been taken care of. In a similar fashion, the Rule of Life is a series of statements by which one lives. It may contain the principles on which one bases life, as well as an outline of daily disciplines to which one is committed. The effort is designed to enable a person to remember, to foster integration of all of life around Christ as the center, and to promote consistency between beliefs and life. A Rule of Life could be a useful tool as the Organizer cultivates faithfulness to the Lord in daily life.

✠ *The spirituality of a loose grip.* However, for balance, the other side should also be noted. Because of the Organizer's tendency toward rigidity with schedules and procedures, it might be important to cultivate the spirituality of a loose grip. By that I mean that as interruptions occur, or as situations arise which prevent the Organizer from following some carefully practiced regimen, it will be important to learn to receive such occasions in a calm spirit. They can be welcomed with the realization that God might have something else in mind than what the Organizer had planned. It may be somewhat like the experience of purchasing a gift for a friend. Perhaps you had in mind getting your friend a conservative brown tie which appealed to you. But before long you came to realize that what your friend really wanted was a western string tie with a steer-horn slide. Out of honor for your friend, you abandoned your original idea and, strange as it seemed, you went gladly down to the Country and Western Shop to buy a string tie! In a similar manner, there may be occasions when what God wants is a string tie with a steer-horn slide, and not the nice, conservative gift which you had planned so carefully to give Him!

The Organizer's Path toward Wholeness

We have noted the infirmities of Organizers and how those might be anticipated. We have also considered ways in which they might naturally nurture their faith. This leads us to this final point. What is the path for spiritual growth for this group?

✠ *Affirm your gifts.* Recognize that your personality type is a distinctive creation gift. You don't have to wish that you had the gifts of another, or bemoan the fact that certain things do not come easily for you. You have traits which are of great value and which need to be invested, as in Jesus' Parable of the Talents. Take a long look at your gifts and practice giving thanks for them. They are not of your own making, but are gifts to be offered back to God for His glory. In the early stages of his life, Solomon had the gift of wisdom and yet humbly recognized that he needed more of it and that God was the source. Allow your gifts to become intensified by the Lord.

✠ *Deny your self-will.* Do not be surprised when the Lord puts you into situations or permits events to unfold where you must do what comes "unnaturally." The Organizer may find himself having to exchange the general's role for that of a foot soldier. She may have to live or work in situations where all routine seems to go out the window and, because of the very nature of things, she has to become flexible and take things as they come. These experiences will try the very fiber of the Organizer's soul! The point is that God either allows or sends us such experiences in order to cause us to reach down and draw from His resources within us and from the body of Christ around us. In such times we are having to die to self-will. We are having to learn to freely surrender our natural desires and inclinations to the Lord. In those experiences we are being carried across our natural thresholds. Since such transcendence is always a possibility in us and in others because of Christ's enabling power, we should never allow a personality profile to define the boundaries of a person's capacities—neither ours nor theirs! God seems to delight in surprising us with the discovery that where we are weak, by His grace we can be made strong!

Through Head to Heart

The wind blows where it wishes, and you hear the sound of it, but cannot tell where it comes from and where it goes. So is everyone who is born of the Spirit. John 3:8

Go out-of-doors, close your eyes, and feel the breeze against your face and listen to the sound of the wind in the trees or across the grasses. Read John 3:1-8 in a whisper.

Imagine yourself in Nicodemus' shoes, from the moment he decided to locate Jesus until he left the Lord and started home again. Try to picture the scene vividly.

Why did Jesus choose to respond in this manner to Nicodemus' simple compliment? Write down the main points Jesus was trying to communicate. What is He trying to say to you?

Tell Jesus how you feel about the words which He has spoken to you. What apologies, resolutions, or gratitude do you need to express?

Chapter Eight

The Analyzers
ISTP and INTP

Analyzers typically appreciate quiet for concentration, prefer a reasoning approach to situations, are oriented toward problem-solving, and don't mind working out the details involved in another's plan.

Because of their more quiet nature, Analyzers do not tend to be outspoken or immediately visible in the community. But their influence is often like the salt in Jesus' image—preserving and flavoring the witness of the church.

Case Study: Matthew

Of all the Gospel writers, we know least about Matthew. We are told that he was a "tax gatherer" before Jesus called him, and that when the call came he immediately "rose and followed Him." We also know that his first action as a new believer seems to have been to host a dinner for his close friends so that they could also meet the Lord. All the rest we must infer from the Gospel which he wrote. But I think that we can discover some significant things from those pages; the profile which emerges illustrates rather clearly some of the essential characteristics of those whom we are calling the Analyzers.

✠ *Matthew was a Jew who joined the Roman civil service to serve them in the tax office.* His neighbors probably considered him a collaborator with the enemy. We don't know why Matthew did this, but evidently he was able to function even in the atmosphere of animosity and resentment which surrounded him. Perhaps he was the kind of man who didn't have to feel loved and appreciated in order to get along in life. In fact, feelings may not have impressed him all that much anyway! We'll come back to that thought again in a moment.

✠ *Matthew's Gospel stands out from the other three because of his great interest in the* teachings *of Jesus.* In fact, if it hadn't been for Matthew, we would not have had the incomparable record of the Sermon on the Mount or the other four signifi-cant chunks of Jesus' teaching which he compiled (the respon-sibilities of the kingdom's leaders in chap. 10; the great para-bles about the kingdom of heaven in chap. 13; the teachings about greatness and forgiveness in the kingdom in chap. 18; and the section about the Final Coming in chaps. 24–25). Mat-thew was a collector of material and, foremost, of Jesus' teachings.

✠ *Matthew was concerned with the inner principles which run through Jesus' teachings.* He was interested in the relation-ship between prophecy and fulfillment, between the Old Cove-nant and the New, between concern for the Jews and the relevance of the Gospel for the whole earth.

✠ *Matthew was neat and tidy in the way he systematized his material.* He often arranged things in groups of threes, fives, or sevens. Such a carefully considered placement made memori-zation easier; with the absence of printed Bibles, memorization of Scripture was a necessity in those early days of the church.

✠ *Matthew was not only full of intellectual curiosity, interest-ed in underlying principles, and able to systematize his material, but he wrote with a mission to convince others, especially fellow Jews, by reasoning with them.* He wanted to demonstrate clearly to them that the prophecies of the Old Testament were fulfilled by Jesus, who, therefore, must be the long-awaited Messiah.

✠ *Matthew may have been rather uninterested or unimpressed with the feeling side of life.* Although he borrowed vast amounts of the Gospel of Mark in compiling his own Gospel, he seems to have deliberately omitted using three fascinating glimpses into Jesus' emotions which were given by Mark (Mark 3:5; 3:12; 10:14). I am aware that there are other valid explanations than this one for his avoidance of the feeling descriptions about Jesus. However, an explanation based on personality characteristics should not be completely overlooked. He simply may have been unaware of the importance that those statements would have for many. So, God used Mark to speak part of the truth, and He used this very different personality—Matthew— to reveal other aspects of Jesus' life.

While these characteristics from Matthew do not give an exhaustive profile of an Analyzer, they do portray some of their most obvious traits. Let's turn to those now for a fuller description of the giftedness of this type of personality.

The Analyzer's Creation Gifts

✠ *Undergirding.* At the outset, Myers notes that the Analyzers use their thinking to "analyze the world, not to run it."[1] Although not incapable of leadership, their natural inclination is toward the kinds of tasks which typically undergird a group. They may be helpful with the preparatory work of research, analysis, and experimentation which must be done in order to assure that the project has a good foundation. Many of them (especially ISTPs) will be carefully patient with details, and, therefore, indispensable to the effectiveness of an undertaking. These are the persons in "mission control" or out on the "pad" preparing for and tracking the launch—but probably not the TV newscasters, the press secretaries, or agency directors who do most of their work in the glare of the lights or in a public arena.

✠ *Reasoning.* Analyzers are thinking types and, therefore, prefer the logical, impersonal, and objective approach in arriving at conclusions and making decisions. They tend to assume that such an approach will be convincing to everyone else too. Therefore, when they present their ideas, they will tend to make their points using just these skills. If someone remains unimpressed, the Analyzer may think that the arguments have not yet been understood and that all that is needed is to say it again, perhaps in a more simplified or amplified fashion. They may be a bit mystified when others express opinions based only on personal values, or when someone seems to put logic aside, making a decision purely out of consideration for the feelings of another person.

✠ *Reserved.* Analyzers generally tend to be reserved and quiet. They may be uncomfortable around persons whom they do not know unless they share a common, compelling interest, such as a hobby or vocation. Matthew's Gospel seems to imply that he invited other tax officers to his "conversion party." His circle of friends was probably (of necessity!) small and tightly knit.

✠ *Committed to truth and justice.* While they certainly are not the only personality type with a deep-seated commitment to these values, this quality is woven into the fabric of the Analyzer. While not usually crusaders for a cause, they will speak up when some boundary has been transgressed, which has led another onto an errant path or into an unjust position. Although they may be reserved, nevertheless, the Analyzers will still try to find a way of sending a clear signal of disagreement and have the inner strength to make a stand, even if there is little support and the stand they take seems to be a maverick one.

The Analyzer's Infirmities

We will deal with three particular vulnerabilities which are likely to be problem areas for Analyzers. They are often the very areas where there already has had to be a considerable amount of confession of sin to God and apology made to others. However, heightened awareness might make it possible for Analyzers to think of ways to anticipate problems and, therefore, to take seriously Jesus' injunction to "watch, lest you enter into temptation."

✠ *Insensitivity.* As thinking types, Analyzers are not naturally oriented toward the feeling side of life. This causes them to come across as rather insensitive—a sore spot to many Analyzers!

An Analyzer had taken a series of steps which caused a coworker (an Enhancer, chap. 10) to feel alienated from the work group. In an ensuing office meeting, when the Analyzer's actions were being discussed, the coworker expressed his hurt. The Analyzer was startled and offended. "But that was not even in my mind!" he retorted, as if unintended repercussions should also be unfelt. He seemed to be saying, "If I didn't *intend* to hurt you, you shouldn't feel hurt!"

There are occasions when Analyzers may know about negative reactions to their ideas or actions, and yet not attempt to reestablish harmony or seek to create a better understanding. Preferring to maintain a rather detached posture, they say in effect, "I don't see why I need to go out of my way to explain my actions or try to win that person over to my side." Matthew may have felt that he had absolutely no need to defend his choice of a profession to his neighbors. The fact that it was selected for logical, personal reasons was probably satisfactory enough for him!

What can they do about their insensitivity? Three things, for starters.

1. They can develop more of an awareness of their own feelings. Because this doesn't come easily, it needs to be practiced. However, the best practice will be in situations where they are not under a great deal of pressure (some crisis, for example) to demonstrate heroic sensitivity toward others.

I've already referred to how we can draw on feelings in prayer and meditation. This will give some valuable practice in speaking personally, not just intellectually, to the Lord. It will also heighten sensitivity to what is actually going on inside, so that names can be given to the feelings noticed. Thinking types of persons often need to become fluent with feeling language.[2]

2. Think about the feelings of others. Why not turn your strength (thinking) into your ally? Use some of your meditation time to focus on persons and the emotions which they may be experiencing. Think of what they have been going through, their distress signals, how certain highly valued aspects of their lives have been either greatly blessed or deeply threatened. Think about the kind of support which they could

use or the kind of affirmation which you could give. Pray for the ministry of God's Spirit to the person. Be quiet before the Lord as you seek to understand what He wants you to do. Then, move from devotion into action.

3. Learn what makes for harmony. Analyzers don't ordinarily require harmonious relationships in order to function well. Aware that another's feelings may have been hurt in some discussion or disagreement, they will often proceed without apology, assuming that others are like themselves and "can get on with it," in spite of what was said. Admittedly, we cannot make everyone happy all the time. And, in fact, there are some persons for whom no amount of apologizing will ever be sufficient to fill the gaping hole in their self-image. However, there are almost always things that we can do to reach out toward another because of our conviction about the importance of the unity of the body of Christ. Disagreements may remain, but inasmuch as possible we will seek to create and maintain a climate of mutual appreciation which will foster community life, even as we work with our conflicting perceptions of some particular situation. One way in which this can be done is to mention what's important and valuable about the other's viewpoint before criticizing it and pushing our own. Another way is to make a careful mental separation between persons and their ideas, so that in our own responses we do not "blow both out of the water."

✠ *Laziness.* Some Analyzers (particularly the ISTPs) have an eye on economy of effort. Myers speaks about this, noting that "this belief can contribute to their efficiency if they judge accurately how much effort is needed and proceed promptly to exert that much effort. However, if they underestimate or underperform, economy of effort can come perilously close to laziness, and little may get done."[3]

To anticipate such an eventuality, it is important for the Analyzer to gather sufficient information on which to accurately assess the labor required in a particular venture. After that, the disciplines of firm goals, established schedules, and structured accountability (for example, reporting on progress to a committee, a friend, or even a spouse) may prove to be valuable aids to assure faithful follow-through.

✠ *Moodiness or emotional explosiveness.* This is often symptomatic of repressed emotions. We all have feelings about our life experiences, but we may not notice or express them. One theory holds that when we ignore our negative feelings, they simply go underground where they continue to simmer. Then the day will come when they surface, often at a rather inopportune time. And when they do, they do so on their own, so to speak. They have their own momentum. They come lashing out or exploding in words that we later regret because of their damaging effects on others and their great embarrassment to us.

The way to deal with this situation is to treat the feeling side of our nature with greater honor and respect. We need to make friends with our emotions and provide positive outlets for their expression. Art and music which involve us can provide healthy occasions for experiencing and expressing a range of feelings, from sadness to joy. They sometimes provide an opportunity to tap latent emotions which we've not dealt with previously.

On the front cover of a publication which I received from my alma mater some years ago, there was a group picture of one of our Marine Corps field units in Vietnam. The troops were dressed in their fatigues, T-shirts, and their dog tags. Underneath was the caption, "Christmas, Da Nang, 1968." I looked at the picture for a while and, surprisingly, tears began to flow. I couldn't understand why. Then I began to remember how different (and safe) my life had been as a seminary student back then. I had carried a lot of guilt inside because I never really had to face the war in which so many my age had died. My grief began to pour out. Only then could I finally begin to deal with this backlog of emotion and trace it to its source in my very real sense of personal guilt.

A picture had become an opening for my feelings and, eventually, for inner healing through God's grace. This leads us to ask the question: How do Analyzers cultivate an awareness and openness to God's grace in their lives?

Natural Ways for Analyzers to Nourish Faith

The words which the Apostle Paul wrote to the church at Philippi ring true for the Analyzers.

> Whatever things are true, whatever things are noble,
> whatever things are just, whatever things are pure,
> whatever things are lovely, whatever things are of
> good report, if there is any virtue and if there is any-
> thing praiseworthy—meditate on these things.
>
> Philippians 4:8

Thinking is the native expression of an Analyzer's spirituality. Let's look at some of the implications of this for the nurture of faith.

✠ *Focusing prayer.* One Saturday evening a few years ago,
an Analyzer friend was already dreading the next morning's
church service. "I just wish the pastor would sum up what he
wants to say on a 3 x 5 card and hand it to us, rather than
putting us through that thirty-minute ordeal!" His humorous
lament was understandable. Analyzers don't like a multitude of
words to get in the way of the point which needs to be made.
They prefer sermons (and writings) which are terse, meaty,
and get right to the heart of the matter. Also, they don't want
to be so flooded with someone else's words that they are
unable to think. Focusing deeply on essential truth nourishes
the faith of an Analyzer.

This focusing is not just for Sunday, however. Time is needed every day for this kind of silent, structured prayer. Such a
daily discipline allows the Analyzers the opportunity to gather
and concentrate their energies and offer themselves freshly to
God. For example, they might take the Lord's Prayer as their
pattern. They can carefully consider the meaning of each
phrase as they pray it slowly, allowing time for thought between each aspect of that prayer. In this way, Jesus' prayer
model can become a meaningful expression of their soul to
God.

✠ *Prayer with feeling language.* The Analyzer will likely
have a heady approach to prayer and may tend to think of God
more as a Grand Concept than as a Living Person. In order to
bring balance, Analyzers will need to become more aware of
their feelings and to use feeling words as they seek to talk
personally with the Father. The use of such feeling language

(to which we have already referred) will enrich their spiritual experience and move them toward their own inner treasure— more about this in a moment.

✠ *Breath prayer.* Some Analyzers have been helped by the use of the "breath prayer," as Ron DelBene has called it.[4] A breath prayer is simply a one-sentence prayer which precisely captures in words one's greatest need at a point in time. This simple sentence will have two parts. It will begin with a name for God which has particular meaning for you and then will identify a quality or gift of God which connects with your greatest perceived need. Often a verse from Scripture will say it best. Here are a few samples of breath prayers.

> "Lord, You are my shepherd;
> guide me in the right paths."
> "Lord, You are my light and my salvation;
> of whom shall I be afraid?"
> "Be Thou my vision, O Christ."
> "Father, help me to live in Your kingdom,
> by Your Power and for Your Glory."

As you spend a few minutes every day, praying those words with meaning, think about what you are saying, and allow your carefully selected sentence to carry your affirmation, bear the full weight of your need, and be an expression of your openness to God. All through the day, at stoplights or while working at some task, you can recall your prayer and breathe it over again and again to God. It is a means of concentrating your attention on eternal truth and allowing God to fill your soul. After a few weeks or months, a different prayer may be more suitable for your situation, so you will select or write another. In order to build your sense of community, you and a friend might share the needs you are experiencing as well as the words to the special breath prayer each of you is using. Then, in your private intercessions for one another, you could pray for your friend in the very words of his or her own prayer.

✠ *Meditation.* A good Bible commentary can enable Analyzers to find the necessary background or provide insight into the details which help illuminate the meaning of a text. It might be useful for them to write out their thoughts, thus capturing the fruit of their reflection. Their gifts can help them simplify complex ideas or sum up the essence of a spiritual principle of life, thus clarifying the passage for themselves— and others! Since they will tend to rely primarily on their cognitive gifts for this, it will be important for them to draw upon their affective side as well. They can do this by asking such questions as these, "What has been the impact of this truth upon my life? How much value do I put upon this particular blessing? How does it make me feel when I realize that God is saying this *to me* or has done this *for me?*"

Above all, each period of meditation needs to bring the Analyzer back into the present moment with a commitment to implement the insights and translate them into personal action. Since Analyzers tend to be a rather private people (as an introvertive group), it might be an important growth discipline for them to find a small group of persons with whom they feel comfortable and with whom they can share at a meaningful level about their spiritual journey.

The Analyzer's Path toward Wholeness

Personal and spiritual growth for the Analyzers will depend upon their readiness to give thanks for their creation gifts and their willingness to lay aside their personal preferences and to cooperate with God's call to more difficult tasks as He presents them. Let's think about what this may mean.

✠ *Affirm your gifts.* Do you remember our case study on Matthew? His interest in the underlying principles of the Gospel of Jesus, his appreciation for Jesus' teaching, his capacity to structure and organize facts, and his ability to convince by reasoning with others were the qualities from which emerged God's special gift to us all—the Gospel which bears Matthew's name and the stamp of his personality. As reserved as he may have been, he not only influenced the close circle of his own friends for Jesus, but God has touched each subsequent generation through him as well. He is the Analyzer's "patron saint"! Give thanks for the special gifts which the Lord has given to you. As you "rise and follow Him" as Matthew did, you bring your creation gifts with you, and the Lord sanctifies them in order to accomplish His purposes through you!

✠ *Deny your self-will.* In the course of following Jesus you will not only be asked to give up the old life, but from time to time you may have to hand over your preferred way of living as well. While you might rather serve in the background, He may call you to take a more active leadership role in some ministry project. While you might favor a more relaxed routine, He may challenge you to set higher goals and to live a more disciplined life so that He can produce greater results through you. While you might opt not to make the effort required to have your ideas accepted, or to foster the harmony which your situation needs, He may give you no peace until you start doing the little or big things which He requires. When God calls us He takes us as we are, but He doesn't leave us there for long!

Wholehearted Understanding

Give me understanding, and I shall keep Your law;
indeed, I shall observe it with my whole heart.

Psalm 119:34

Read Psalm 119:33-40 aloud softly, listening to the sound of
the words as you read. Underline any thoughts or phrases
which strike you with their beauty or power.

Notice any pictures, scenes, or memories which these verses
evoke within you. Imagine how your life might look if you
lived out the reality of this passage.

What have you been tempted to covet? (v. 36) What are some
of the worthless things which have held your attention? What
does it mean to observe God's law with a whole heart? List the
promises which the psalmist makes to God.

How do you feel about making such promises today? Visualize
the Lord present with you and talk with Him as your dearest
friend.

Chapter Nine

The Encouragers
ESFJ and ENFJ

Encouragers are noted for their conscientiousness, tact, and personal warmth. They are deeply loyal and devoted, and have the capacity for true empathy with others. They are at their best when they feel that their possessions are in order and their relationships in harmony.

Case Study: Ruth

Of the several biblical figures who exemplify characteristics of the Encouragers, Ruth could be taken as a kind of prototype. Her outstanding personal qualities have been immortalized in the wedding ceremony of many denominations, where her famous lines are quoted.

> Entreat me not to leave you,
> or to turn back from following after you;
> for wherever you go, I will go;
> and wherever you lodge, I will lodge;
> your people shall be my people,
> and your God, my God.
>
> Ruth 1:16

Ruth, a young Moabite woman, spoke these beautiful words to her Jewish mother-in-law, sometime in the middle of the twelfth century B.C.

During a time of famine, a man named Elimelech had

brought his little Judean family south into the country of Moab. Here the small band struggled to eke out an existence by farming. Their hard work paid off and the family not only survived, but even found unexpected happiness. Both of Elimelech's sons fell in love with local Moabite girls. History doesn't record their discussions of the matter, but it could not have been easy for the family to part from the strict Jewish law which forbade intermarriage with Moabite people. However, their experience in this foreign country created a climate for acceptance. Here in Moab they found a welcome. The land provided them with sustenance, and now their sons even found love. An exception to the law must have seemed justified to them. That's how Ruth and Orpah came to be family members.

As time passed, the land took its toll on Elimelech's family as he and both of his sons died. Naomi, his wife, suddenly found her pleasant fortunes had turned bitter through tragedy. With no one to support her, she urged her daughters-in-law to return to their own families as she made her long journey home again. It was at this point that Ruth, clinging to Naomi, spoke her famous words. Let's take a closer look at the qualities of this special woman.

✠ *Courageous and responsible.* Imagine the courage it must have taken for Ruth, still a young lady with so much of life before her, to trade all that was familiar in preference for an enemy land of strange customs and with laws which forbade its people from mixing with her kind. Think of the deep sense of personal responsibility which she showed when she committed herself to care for Naomi. If her mother-in-law had no one who could look after her, then Ruth certainly would never abandon this woman whom she respected, admired, and loved. She determined to be their breadwinner. Ruth exemplifies the Encourager's courageous sense of personal responsibility.

✠ *Considerate and conscientious.* Ruth's bond with Naomi went so deep that she was willing to identify with her as completely as possible. Ruth not only left her land and people, but from that day forth, even made Naomi's God her own. Such selfless generosity, especially in light of the prevailing customs of that day, is hard for us to imagine!

When they arrived at Naomi's home in Bethlehem of Judea, Ruth saw their immediate and very practical needs. She took responsibility for collecting their food by the ancient practice of *gleaning*, the right of the needy to pick up the stray stalks of grain left after the reapers had finished in the fields. We are told that she worked hard from morning until evening, with little time for rest (Ruth 2:7).

One day, through a remarkable series of circumstances, Ruth was invited to dine at the home of Boaz, the owner of the field. Ruth made sure that she collected enough food at the feast to take back home to Naomi so that she could share this blessing as well.

Ruth even surrendered her life to what must have seemed to her a strange Jewish tradition, by which the nearest of kin could act as the *goel* or redeemer of the property and family of a relative whose widow was left impoverished. In Naomi's case, after the default of the next-of-kin, the right of *goel* fell to Boaz. One evening Ruth went to Boaz to ask for his help in this way, knowing that she would be taken into his household if he consented.

Such a sense of personal duty and sacrificial thoughtfulness for the needs of others is not unusual in the actions of Encouragers.

✠ *Faithful and devoted.* When Ruth decided to follow the Lord of Israel, her natural gifts and disposition became a fresh witness to God's grace. Boaz was struck by the *loving* quality of her faith. By using words almost identical to Genesis 12:1 (Ruth 2:11), he seems to have made a conscious connection between Ruth's "venture of love" in coming to Judea and Abraham's "venture of faith" in leaving all and heading out to a land which God would show him. Boaz linked Ruth's loving decision and her faith in the Lord by noting that she launched out into the unknown, casting herself upon "the Lord God of Israel, under whose wings you have come for refuge" (Ruth 2:12). There is also an interesting connection between the words *holiness* and *kindness* (Ruth 3:10). Either word can be used to translate the Hebrew expression used in that text. Ruth's *holiness* was evident in her willingness to place herself under God's law regarding the *goel.* When *kindness* is used to translate the verse, we see by implication that Ruth's holiness is demonstrated by her kindness in that she chose Boaz over the many eligible men who were more her own age.

Encouragers are often people who, when their blend of personal traits are dedicated to the Lord, live out a faith which can best be described as a journey of love. Their holiness is often gloriously displayed by their kindness to others.

The Encourager's Creation Gifts

There are three sets of gifts, some of them we have already observed in Ruth, which seem to especially characterize Encouragers: warmth and hospitality, loyalty and idealism, and practicality and responsibility.[1] As with other types, every Encourager may not exhibit each characteristic, but this set of qualities does help us to identify the group as a whole.

✠ *Warmth and hospitality.* Encouragers take a personal view of just about everything. It is especially evident in their capacity to identify and empathize with others. For this reason they can pick up on cues and notice things which other types of personalities might never see. The ESFJ remembers these details, fits them together, and seems to understand what others need without having to be told. The ENFJ is capable of reading between the lines and intuiting needs and possibilities. Encouragers apparently come equipped with a "compassion radar." They not only pick up the "need blips" on their mental screen, but also seem able to respond thoughtfully, as if by instinct. The telephone call, a cheery card, a little gift, a visit over coffee become instruments of their care. They often seem to have just the right words for the occasion, words which flow without rehearsal or forethought. Encouragers genuinely like people, desire the happiness of others, and greatly prize harmony in all their relationships.

✠ *Loyalty and idealism.* It would be hard to find a group more fiercely loyal than the Encouragers. Their family and their friends can count on them. They tend to be admiring rather than critical, especially when it comes to those who are in authority. They often have a special place in their hearts for their leaders (pastors, teachers, public officials). Their deep, personal ideals form the basis of their daily life. When someone they admire betrays the Encouragers' personal ideals, their pain is deep and their memory can be permanent.

Encouragers are great supporters and protectors of the institutions which perpetuate their values. Their church, school, and community organizations would be lost without them!

✠ *Practicality and responsibility.* Encouragers—especially the ESFJs—often evidence their capacity for a common sense which enables them to discern obvious needs to which they respond. They don't make a great deal of fuss over their actions, but do appreciate when another recognizes what they've done. The reason that they don't like to call attention to their actions is that they tend to feel that the very ordinary nature of their response renders their action commonplace. They certainly do not see it as heroic. "I only did what had to be done" or "I only did what anyone would have done" are not unusual reactions.

What is heroic is that Encouragers *do* what others often just *think* about doing! I often feel that while I may be good in *theory*, my Encourager wife is good in *practice*! We all know which is better in the Lord's sight!

Duty is an important concept for Encouragers, for they approach life with a sense of personal obligation. We've already noted their support for the institutions of society and their loyalty to others. Of course, as others quickly learn this open "secret" about them, they keep handing them things to do. Since no one else will take the job, Encouragers end up bearing the weight of many expectations. Because of their many obligations, they may feel unable to live up to their own inner demands and may postpone meeting their own personal needs until some more convenient time. When they are so overloaded, their "gift" has become an infirmity. Realizing this may prevent us from taking advantage of them or from taking them for granted. At the same time, we can understand that while Encouragers may need to say no more often, others around them need to say yes.

Encouragers' practicality and responsibility are evidenced

not only by the way they deal personally with people, but also in that their personal approach carries over to their possessions as well. They care *about* material things and like to keep them in working order, polished, oiled, and organized. When their things are out of place, they feel personally out of balance. Encouragers' surroundings are important to them. They may appreciate a space which is not only neat, but also warmly decorated. Often they evidence a personal touch in arranging their living or work area. Pictures of loved ones and meaningful mementos may have a special place, personalizing their environment as well as providing aesthetic appeal.

The Encourager's Infirmities

✠ *Hypersensitivity.* Because other people matter so much to them, Encouragers may have a difficult time saying no to others' requests for help. They do not want to disappoint people, increase burdens, or see others discomforted when there is something more that could be done for them. This oversensitivity to others often belies an insensitivity to their own needs and limitations. As a result, Encouragers' personal effectiveness may be diminished.

In chapter 1, we noted how Jesus modeled an important balance in this regard. He showed that it is all right to acknowledge our limitations and to care for our personal needs. He demonstrated this by withdrawing from the increasing demands of the crowds in order to cultivate a necessary solitude, find rest, and spend time in prayer.

Hypersensitivity renders Encouragers vulnerable to criticism, confrontation, and relational difficulties. Rather than dealing with such things objectively by using the analytical or thinking side, they tend to deal with them subjectively, taking them deeply and personally. They may brood over personal hurt resulting from a disagreement, a negative evaluation, or a sharp remark until it creates an inner infection of the soul (perhaps evidenced by depression or self-denigrating thoughts). Such complications may make it more difficult for Encouragers to bounce back than it is for many other personality types. Of course, such hypersensitivity may also make it hard for these persons to receive constructive criticism or to use conflict redemptively.

In anticipation of such a weakness, the Encourager might deliberately practice methods of gaining psychological distance from painful personal events, in order to become more objective about upsetting incidents. Some find it helpful to write out their experiences in a personal notebook, utilizing their best analytical skills to interpret an episode. Most will find even more help in talking things out with a personal confidant. The understanding attention of a *trusted* friend is almost indispensable for the healing of many personal hurts.

✠ *Unreflective action.* We have extolled the capacity of Encouragers for insight and understanding which leads them into caring action. However, we must also record the flip side as well. Because of their tendency to act without much reflection and to place more weight on their feeling reactions before sufficient examination of the evidence, Encouragers may react to situations in ill-considered or even counterproductive ways. For example, dependent, manipulative people can hook into Encouragers' natural sympathy in order to gain the attention and assistance which they desire. We have all struggled with the realization that there are some occasions when it is actually in the other person's best interest for us to say no to some requests; we need to choose those responses which promote the other's self-sufficiency and support their growth toward maturity rather than continuing to encourage immature dependency. This might be an important insight for Encourager parents whose sense of personal duty may make it hard for them to share family duties. Such delegation of tasks could, in fact, help to cultivate a sense of shared responsibility which is important for the growth of each member of the family "team."

✠ *Avoidance of unpleasantness.* The Encourager prefers harmony and good feelings. Sometimes this causes a blind spot when it comes to disagreeable situations, unpleasant facts, or disconcerting thoughts. This weakness touches many areas of an Encourager's life, including the spiritual life.

For example, they may try to avoid the discomfort of honest doubt or the challenging work of thinking through their faith, choosing instead to cling to an unreflective, sentimental approach to the spiritual life. Paul may have been thinking of such a tendency when he wrote to the people of Colossae that he wanted them to be filled with courage, drawn together in love, developing the wealth of assurance which could only come through true understanding and knowledge (Colossians 2:2). Such an understanding faith is always fed by hard thinking, and by a willingness to wrestle through doubts and ponder books of spiritual substance which challenge the mind and enable us to lay more firm foundations of knowledge about God's work through Christ.

Feeling-oriented persons, including the Encourager, may be tempted to settle for a subjective approach to faith which, in the final analysis, is growth-stunting. It is not unusual for a person with an intensely subjective spiritual life to eventually experience almost overpowering doubts in the midst of life's storms. Such a person might feel overcome, with the sinking fear that beliefs of many years might, in the final analysis, turn out to be wishful thinking, self-deception, childish fantasy, or tragic illusion.[2] Abiding assurance and profound conviction are achieved by what John Wesley called the "conjoining of knowledge and vital piety." This is always the best path for growth.

Natural Ways for Encouragers to Nourish Faith

✠ *Communal spirituality.* The old adage "No one can be a Christian alone" is true for all of us. However, none realize this more quickly and poignantly than Encouragers. Their spiritual lives are nurtured through sharing relationships with brothers and sisters in the faith. This can be done in countless ways.

In our area, a group of young mothers have formed what they call their "Galatians 6:2 Group." They meet together regularly for a fellowship meal, sharing, and prayer. They begin at 6 in the evening and leave about midnight. They are discovering the power of Paul's injunction, "Bear one another's burdens and so fulfill the law of Christ." A group of men joins together for breakfast early every Saturday morning at the church. It is their opportunity to laugh together and talk about the week just passed, look at the challenges ahead, to celebrate victories, and to pray for guidance. A group of men from a Sunday School class have now extended their fellowship beyond Sunday morning to whitewater rafting and fishing expeditions as ways of enjoying their fellowship together. As a result, when any one of them is going through a particularly difficult time, it is not unusual for him to call the others for counsel and prayer.

✠ *Spirituality of compassion.* There are several stories in Scripture where we are told how persons who showed compassion to the stranger were astonished to discover that it was actually the Lord or one of His angels in disguise. Such stories remind us of the way that spirituality and compassion are wedded together. Encouragers can teach us much about this through their spirituality of compassion. They discover that the way into the Lord's presence is along the royal road of kindness and hospitality. When going through spiritually dry times or periods of discouragement, it is vital for Encouragers to become involved in practical ministry—unless, of course, that dryness is a result of the depletion of physical and emotional reserves from excessive service. We will return to this thought in the next section.

✠ *Prayer of the heart.* Encouragers seem to know instinctively about what the saints called "affective prayer." When they pray, it is natural for them to speak from the heart to the Lord, expressing their feelings of love, trust, praise, or sorrow to Him.

✠ *Devotional aids.* Their gift of feeling enables Encouragers to identify with characters in Gospel stories. They are able to link their own experiences of joy, fear, gratitude, or loneliness with similar feelings in the stories. This enables them to enter into the Gospel and hear Christ's words with special, personal meaning.

Their knack for personalizing their environment may be employed meaningfully in worship as well. They may find it helpful to set up a worship center for their daily devotions. My wife once combined a picture of the sea, some seashells, and our family's pet goldfish to transform a section of kitchen cabinets into a beautiful spot of this kind.

Encouragers are often lovers of books, and stories about

people with whom they can identify may prove very helpful for their growth. Likewise, they often especially appreciate structured devotional guides (for example, a brief Scripture and devotional interpretation, a personal story, a practical application to daily life, and a prayer suggestion).

Finally, Encouragers appreciate sermons which touch the heart and which include examples from real life to which they can relate. It is not that they want to be entertained, but that they need the kind of encouragement they are so good at providing for others.

The Encourager's Path toward Wholeness

✠ *Affirm your gifts.* It is important that Encouragers affirm their gifts. Sometimes they sell themselves short, feeling that there is little particularly noteworthy about their service to others. Actually their kindness is the central core of Christ's ethic. Their person-centered lives are a refreshing antidote to much of the depersonalization around us. Their genuine enjoyment and sense of responsibility for others often provide us with strength and can seem like the glue which holds so many valuable institutions together!

✠ *Deny your self-will.* The pathway of growth for Encouragers must include the surrender of impossible idealism. They need to accept the fact that they cannot take personal responsibility for everyone else's happiness, nor can they control the amount of goodwill shown by persons around them. A more honest appraisal of human nature in the light of Scripture might enable them to move in the direction of Christian realism and help them develop a more objective perception of people and groups. Along with their warmth of heart, they need to develop that inner toughness which will enable them to go on functioning effectively even when relationships are not going perfectly.

A genuine appreciation of their humanness may enable them to acknowledge their limits and to be as kind to themselves as they are to others.

Finally, they may need to grow in a personal objectivity which will enable them to receive the critique of others and grow from it, realizing that such experiences, while difficult, are not necessarily bad. The story of Jesus, Mary, and Martha is full of meaning for spiritual growth. Mary was in the sitting room talking with Jesus. Meanwhile, Martha, upset over all the work she had to do, said, "Lord, do You not care that my sister has left me to serve alone? Therefore tell her to help me." To which Jesus replied, "Martha, Martha! You are worried and troubled about many things. But one thing is needed, and Mary has chosen that good part" (Luke 10:41-42). We are not told how Martha responded at that moment. Did she go to the kitchen and cry because her feelings were hurt? Did she feel stung by Jesus' criticism and become self-deprecating, feeling that no one really understood her? Or did she, on hearing His words, find the grace to accept them and to grow? It may have been the most important moment of her life!

Perceiving and Receiving

*We have received ... the Spirit which is from God, that
we might understand the gifts bestowed on us by God.*
1 Corinthians 2:12, RSV

———————————————————

Read 1 Corinthians 2:6-16 aloud twice. First, in its entirety,
listening to the words. Second, pausing at each place where
Paul speaks of something God has given, planned, or done for
us.

Draw a box in which you write words or sketch symbols representing some of the intangible "gifts bestowed on us by God."

What did you think about those intangible gifts before the
Spirit opened your eyes to them? Have you ever lost sight of
some of these gifts and ceased living in their reality? How has
God renewed them in you? What difference has it made?

Express to God your feelings about these gifts which you've
named. Talk to Him about your desires for deeper understanding, appreciation, and reverence for these blessings.

Chapter Ten

The Enhancers
ISFP and INFP

Enhancers are noted for their quiet warmth and their genuine optimism. Their presence graces the relational atmosphere. Although they may be reticent to make claims for themselves, their contributions of practical helpfulness and shared insight often prove invaluable.

Case Study: Luke

The author of the third Gospel, which bears his name, was a Greek-speaking Gentile. He was among the best educated of the New Testament writers and worked as a physician before he became a fellow traveler with Paul on the early missionary journeys which emblazoned a trail for the Gospel through the Mediterranean region. He became the movement's best historian and was a confidant to the Apostle Paul, whose feelings about him are obvious from his warm descriptions calling Luke, a "fellow laborer" and the "beloved physician." In fact, when Paul wrote his last letter before his martyrdom in Rome, he included the touching note, "Only Luke is with me" (2 Timothy 4:11).

From a study of Luke's writings we can identify several of the qualities we usually associate with Enhancers. Let's look at some of these now.

✠ *Mission and purpose.* Because of Luke's deep friendship with Paul and his relationships with almost all of the leaders in the first-century church, including many of the eyewitnesses to Christ who were still living, and because of his firsthand knowledge of the key geographical centers of the new movement, Luke was in a special position to collect information about Jesus. He also had a unique vantage point from which to view the impact of the Christ-event upon the world. Luke knew that this was not a treasure to be hoarded, but a gift to share. He donated his gift to the glory of the Lord. To Theophilus, the high-ranking citizen who would actually receive the manuscript of his Gospel, and through him to the wider circle who would read it, Luke speaks of the overriding purpose which governed his writing.

> Inasmuch as many have taken in hand to set in order a narrative of those things which are most surely believed among us, just as those who from the beginning were eyewitnesses and ministers of the word delivered them to us, it seemed good to me also, having had perfect understanding of all things from the very first, to write to you an orderly account, most excellent Theophilus, that you may know the certainty of those things in which you were instructed.   Luke 1:1-4

Enhancers typically look beyond the deeds of the present moment to the larger context of their meaning in order to identify the purposes which they are serving.

✠ *Humility and self-restraint.* We know that Luke was no spectator; he was a chief actor in the events which he records in the Book of Acts. And yet we are struck by his remarkable self-restraint, since he does not describe his own personal exploits nor display any of his notable achievements. He always seems to keep himself in the background, preferring to throw the spotlight directly on the Lord (in Luke) and on what the Lord did through the apostles (in Acts). His self-effacing style is evident in his writing.[1] Such a modest and unassuming manner is often typical of Enhancers.

✠ *Tenderness and compassion.* Luke not only intended that his work would provide a reliable account of Christ's words and deeds for the undergirding of faith, but it is also apparent that he wrote the Gospel with a passion that *all* people would come to know the Lord. Luke's record is filled with stories which make it clear that the Good News was for pagans as well as the religious, for the Gentiles as well as Jews, for women as well as men, for the poor as well as the rich, for the outcasts as well as those who were respectable.

In the light of our own contemporary situation, it is particularly important to notice Luke's concern and compassion for women. He tells about the widow of Nain (7:11-17), the unnamed woman who was saved by Jesus (7:36-50), the women who followed and served the Lord (8:1-3), the story of Mary and Martha (10:38-42), the women weeping before the cross (23:27), and the women from Galilee who were present for Jesus' burial (23:55). The importance of Luke's record concerning these women and their place in the Gospel story cannot be minimized, especially when we consider the place of women in the culture of his day. It is an indication of Luke's sensitivity and compassion, traits which are common in Enhancers.

✠ *Artistry of expression.* We have already noted that Luke was an educated man. This fact is obvious when we study the style of his writing. In this regard, he was the best of the New Testament writers. His work is polished Greek literature.

His artistry is evident in the word pictures which he paints. He gave us such unforgettable descriptions of situations and portraits of personalities that they have continued to inspire great paintings down through the centuries. Who could ever forget his beautifully direct way of capturing Jesus' Parables of the Good Samaritan or of the Prodigal Son? How could we ever hear news reports from Jerusalem again without recalling Luke's account of how Jesus "drew near . . . saw the city, and wept over it, saying, 'If you had known, even you, especially in this your day, the things that make for your peace! But now they are hidden from your eyes' " (19:41-42). Who could fail to form a vivid mental image of the gripping scene in Gethsemane as Luke portrays how Jesus "in agony . . . prayed more earnestly. And His sweat became like great drops of blood falling down to the ground" (22:24).

Luke offers a good example, even if somewhat exaggerated, of the qualities of articulation and expression which we often discover in Enhancers.

✠ *Attraction to prayer and retreat.* More than any of the other Gospel writers, Luke records occasions when Jesus withdrew to pray. In Luke 5:16, he not only tells us of the demands for Jesus' ministry (as the other writers do), and the fact that He retreated to lonely places (as Mark had also pointed out), but amplifies it by noting that He went out into lonely places where He *prayed.* Luke is the only Gospel writer to explain that Jesus spent an entire night in prayer before choosing the twelve disciples. He is the only one to record that it was "one day when Jesus was praying alone" that the disciples came to Him and He asked them, "Who do men say that I am?" Only Luke says specifically that it was when Jesus took the disciples up on a hillside *to pray* that He was gloriously transfigured before their eyes. Luke alone places Jesus' teaching about the Lord's Prayer in the context of His own prayertime, which was interrupted by the disciples' request for help in knowing how to pray. Finally, Luke is the one who observed that when Jesus predicted Peter's denial He also added, "But I have prayed for you, Simon, that your faith will not fail."

We would never claim that Enhancers pray more than any other type. However, there does seem to be an inner disposition which makes withdrawal and the inner life especially attractive and appealing to them.

The Enhancer's Creation Gifts

Some of the Enhancer's creation gifts have already emerged in our case study. Now we'll turn to a more careful examination of the special traits of this type of personality.

✠ *Mission and purpose.* One Enhancer said in a group, "My work is important to me as long as I feel a sense of mission about it. When I do, I am passionate. But when I lose that perspective, feeling fades, work becomes drudgery, and I start looking around for my niche somewhere else!" It was a perfect illustration of Myers' observation,

> They are twice as good when working at a job they believe in; their feeling puts added energy behind their

> efforts. They want their work to contribute to something that matters to them—human understanding or happiness or health, or perhaps the perfecting of some project or undertaking. They want a purpose behind their paycheck, no matter how big the paycheck.[2]

✠ *Warmth and quiet reserve.* By their kind disposition, gentle spirit, and positive regard, they seem to radiate goodwill when they are around others. This gives them the special quality of personal presence which I have tried to tag by the label Enhancer. For they do have a manner which graces our lives in a special way when they are with us. However, when it comes to feelings, it is usually difficult to tell from surface appearances just how deeply Enhancers may care about a situation. They consider their deepest feelings to be personal material to be shared very judiciously.

There is an old saying, "Gentleness is the strongest thing in the world." There is great truth in that adage, and the Enhancers' strength in relationships and their ability to win the cooperation of others is often apparent. However, their gentleness sometimes leaves them vulnerable to being taken advantage of. In the hills of eastern Kentucky, there is another proverb, "The meek shall inherit the earth, but not its mineral rights!"

✠ *Optimism and hope.* "You can't keep a good man down" must have been said about an Enhancer. They seem to have a genuine optimism and enthusiasm about their mission in life; however dim the situation, they seem utterly convinced that it will work out "because it is right." This characteristic often carries over into their work with people, especially in counseling. They tend to have a positive regard for people, and a deep-seated belief in others' capacities or possibilities. Perhaps it is their subtle, even unconscious, communication of such confidence in other people's inner strengths which sometimes makes the Enhancer an effective counselor and source of healing.

✠ *Independence and perfectionism.* The fact that feeling is their dominant mental function means that Enhancers are value-driven people. At the same time, the fact that they are intro-vertive reminds us that their values tend to be personally derived, and not usually fashioned out of interchange with oth-ers. This gives Enhancers a very independent streak; it also means that they are continually using their own measure to assess their personal accomplishments and actions. It is not unusual for Enhancers to be plagued with feelings of inadequa-cy or failure because of the great gaps which they perceive between their personal ideals and their actual performance.[3] Enhancers tend to put much higher value on self-consistency and inner faithfulness than on outer signs of success, or on how much they are able to impress others.

✠ *Flexibility and openness.* Enhancers usually approach life in a flexible and relaxed manner. They are not typically agenda-driven, but are able to adapt to situations as they unfold. They seem to have higher expectations of themselves than they have of other people. They are open and receptive to other people and their views until those views run counter to one of their own cherished personal values.[4] At that point their tendons tighten, and Enhancers can become remarkably stubborn and inflexible.

I'll never forget seeing a very tolerant Enhancer become adamant about an injustice being done in a certain situation. His eyes flashed as he stood before us, forcefully stating his conviction and calling for a reversal of a committee action. It was such a contrast to his usual demeanor, and yet so consis-tent with his compassionate disposition, that the stunned and sobered group not only gave him their undivided attention but took the desired action as well! By their response they were practically saying, "If he feels that strongly about this matter, then we *must* be wrong!"

The Enhancer's Infirmities

There are three particular weaknesses to which Enhancers are especially susceptible—feelings of inadequacy, resistance to reason, and reluctance to share personally.

✠ *Feelings of inadequacy.* It is possible for Enhancers to have such idealistic expectations of themselves that they not only fail to achieve those standards, but often feel guilt about such failure and about their inadequacy for service to Christ. Let's examine this vulnerability more closely.

On those occasions when they fail to meet some unrealistic expectation they have for themselves they become painfully aware of a great gap between the ideal and the real. When the issue is relational or ministry-related, instead of realistically assessing their actions or examining the appropriateness of their goals, their knee-jerk reaction may be self-depreciation for not having done the thing as well as it *should* have been done, or not having responded to a person as they *ought* to have. Such thoughts lead to feelings of guilt which, in turn, undermine confidence and become a vicious circle.

The way to break the chain may ultimately be a spiritual process which makes use of self-knowledge. Two things are required. First, they will need to make an intentional decision not to remain in their introvertive mode, but to come out of themselves and seek others for conversation and sharing. I want to emphasize the *intentional* nature of this decision; their natural tendency is to turn inward, and that is the last thing Enhancers need to do in such moods as these!

The second requirement is for them to take another look at the facts as well as at the deeper levels of meaning in their circumstances. For example, they may recognize that their idealistic expectations (for self or others) are more akin to wistful yearnings for the heavenly city than as goals appropriate to the human condition.

They will need to be recalled to the Gospel, by remembering that the inner conflict they experience is not the total reality, since we live under *grace*. Christ has redeemed us and God has accepted us, not on the basis of our successes but because of His love. Personal frailties and failures don't disqualify us for ministry; rather, they dispose us for the Lord's grace, and our utter dependence upon grace authenticates ministry. It is not our need of grace but our refusal or rejection of it which represents true failure.

Enhancers' feelings of inadequacy stem not only from the failure to measure up to their own ideals, but frequently result when they engage in comparisons between themselves and other personality types. Enhancers often feel overshadowed when they are around confident extroverts, and their sense of insecurity can be stirred up when they are in the presence of strong Thinking types, like the Organizers and Analyzers. On such occasions, because they are having to relate out of less-used functions in themselves, their sense of inadequacy arises. Once again, the breakthrough seems to come from the blending of self-discovery and spiritual awareness. Our differences from one another are not deficiencies. *Each one* has been blessed with a unique blending of spiritual and creational gifts which result in special contributions to the body of Christ. "Each one" is an important biblical concept.

> There are varieties of gifts, but the same Spirit; and there are varieties of service, but the same Lord; and there are varieties of working, but it is the same God who inspires them all in every one. *To each* is given the manifestation of the Spirit for the common good.
> 1 Corinthians 12:4-7, RSV, italics added

We do not need to regret being born with one personality type rather than another. Instead, Scripture challenges us to discover and celebrate our mutual contributions, and to become more accepting of ourselves and unified with others through fellowship, service, and worship.

✠ *Resistance to reason.* Myers notes that it is possible for people of this type to make good use of their Thinking function in order to win support for their causes. However, Enhancers will never allow their Thinking function to oppose their *own* Feeling decisions.[5] She probably overstated it, but not by much!

Enhancers can be very self-critical with regard to how they measure up to their own ideals, but can at the same time remain remarkably uncritical of the very notions and ideals which drive them. As a result, others may view Enhancers' actions as arbitrary, impulsive, and without sufficient grounds, and feel that they simply plunge ahead, without even stopping to consider that their actions may be ill-advised.

✠ *Reluctance to share personally.* The Enhancers' private nature and independent streak lead us to a third area of potential vulnerability. They often keep their own feelings tucked away on the inside to such an extent that others may feel they never really know them. When the stresses and pressures of life build up or their own anger begins to simmer, Enhancers are likely to become even more silent. That means that if they do turn loose, they may have built up quite a head of steam. It is very important to their own well-being for Enhancers to develop trusted friendships where personal sharing can take place.

As marriage partners and as parents, Enhancers would do well to remember that those who are dear to them not only appreciate the warmth and kindness of their actions, but draw strength and develop closeness with them as the Enhancers verbalize personal feelings as well.

It sometimes happens that positive experiences of sharing with a trusted few can free Enhancers for relating more personally with an even larger number. Such personal growth is important since it enables their light to emerge from under the basket (where it has been so carefully protected) and give illumination to a wider sphere. God's good gifts to us are always meant to be shared!

Natural Ways for Enhancers to Nourish Faith

✠ *Personalizing Scripture.* Because of their personal nature, Enhancers will find that they are able to get most from Scripture when they take sufficient time to live with a passage and make it their own. They will be especially helped either by taking a few verses a day and pondering them deeply, or spending an entire week with just three or four passages.

Some denominations use a lectionary to guide the church through a yearly cycle of readings which carry them through the various themes of Scripture and celebrations of the church. These lectionary readings (usually four each week: a Psalm, Old Testament reading, Gospel reading, and another New Testament passage) can prove to be a very helpful devotional guide for the Enhancers. The amount of Scripture may be about right, and by reading these passages with the rest of their denomination, they will be strengthened by a sense of companionship on the spiritual journey.

Learning Scripture by heart is another way God's Word can come alive for Enhancers. The discipline is a tough one, but the rewards are great. Rehearsal of special verses, mulling over their personal implications, and turning them into prayers for ourselves (or others) all through the day and night become ways that we can practice dwelling in the Word and allowing the Word to dwell in our hearts.

✠ *The spiritual journal.* We have seen the usefulness of the journal for other personality types; it also has its place for Enhancers. Because they are not typically verbal about their feelings, they can use the journal as a place to write about life events or inner struggles and to articulate the emotions which are a part of those experiences. This may give the Enhancers exercise in objectivity, a quality they often lack. The feelings and thoughts which emerge through these writings can then be incorporated into conversational prayer or written letter-prayers so that the journal becomes an aid to faith development. This process may also enable them to be aware and expressive of their internal dynamics, in order that they might share these things more freely with those closest to them. Of course, the danger is that Enhancers may use their journal as a substitute for relationships. Such a temptation needs to be zealously avoided.

✠ *Listening or discerning prayer.* Enhancers often find prayer and the inner life especially appealing. Their prayer life will probably be characterized by personal conversation with the Lord, or by entering with feeling into the written prayers of others. They might find listening or discerning prayer of particular help. By this I mean that after pouring out their own feelings to God, they need to become quiet and still, attentive to what it is that the Lord may be trying to communicate to them. As this discipline is incorporated into their lives, they may be astonished at the results. Often they will experience piercing insights, evocative images, ideas to be acted on; or they may recall Scripture verses which they do not even remember memorizing. When these things happen, it is important to take note of them, test their validity by sharing them with a spiritual friend, and act on whatever truth has been revealed.

Of course, we all know (sometimes too well!) those agonizing experiences when we want some word from the Lord, plead for it, and wait for it, but experience only a deafening silence! What do we do then? When such time comes, don't turn away from God in disappointment or despair, but stay with Him and tell Him how the silence feels. It is often in the midst of enshrouding clouds, when God "feels" so absent, that our faith can grasp the Lord most profoundly and, with spiritual insight, we can see our true selves most vividly.

The Enhancer's Path toward Wholeness

✠ *Affirm your gifts.* It is essential for growth that Enhancers move from self-consciousness toward Christ-consciousness and ministry-orientated living. Perhaps you've found yourself to be most self-conscious during those times when you were preoccupied with feelings of inadequacy. By intensifying your life of prayer, you can learn to focus your attention more on the Lord. You can practice acknowledging and giving Him thanks for the specific creation gifts and spiritual gifts with which you have been blessed. As you recognize their true Source, you are also realizing that what you have received needs to be surrendered for the Lord's purposes. Gifts are for the giving.

✠ *Deny your self-will.* Prayer and retreat are vital experiences as long as they lead to personal transparency before God and to responsible relationships with others. Unfortunately, they can also be used as means of avoidance rather than encounter. Symptoms of such misuse are inaccessibility and unavailability. For Enhancers, growth requires a movement from isolation to relationship. You may need to recall this truth especially during times when disillusionment with yourself or others makes withdrawal from Christian community seem a valid alternative. In fact, those occasions when your illusions have been shattered may contain within them a hidden invitation for you to discover the true meaning of Christian fellowship. Only disenchantment can prepare us to appreciate the profound difference between *social camaraderie* which usually depends on others living up to our expectations, and *spiritual fellowship* which is based on our mutual need for the forgiving love of God through Christ.[6]

Finally, if you are an Enhancer, your growth may also be linked to your movement from perfectionism to grace. You may discover that the Lord is calling to you in the midst of your feelings of failure, asking you to surrender your self-imposed, unrealistic standards and to let Him be God for you. He may be inviting you to live under His rule of love, rather than under the tyranny of an overdemanding conscience.

> Little children, let us not love [merely] in theory or in speech but in deed and in truth—in practice and in sincerity. By this we shall come to know—perceive and recognize and understand—that we are of the Truth, and can reassure (quiet, conciliate, and pacify) our hearts in His presence in whatever our hearts in [tormenting] self-accusation make us feel guilty and condemn us. For [we are in God's hands]; He is above and greater than our consciences (our hearts), and He knows (perceives and understands) everything—nothing is hidden from Him.
>
> 1 John 3:18-20, AMP

Set Free

But when Jesus saw her, He called her to Him and said to her, "Woman, you are loosed from your infirmity."
Luke 13:12

Read Luke 13:10-17 in a whisper. Re-create the details of the setting in your mind and allow your senses to convey the impressions of sight, sound, touch, and smell. Stay with the passage until it is vivid for you.

Imagine yourself in the place of the woman. Envision what it is like for Jesus to recognize you. What infirmity has been particularly burdensome and binding for you? What do Jesus' words and touch mean to you?

List the contrasts which are contained in this passage. Compare the religious issue raised with the spiritual principle which Jesus enunciated. How is this principle relevant for us today?

Talk personally with Christ about your weaknesses and His love. Allow Him to show you the way in which you face your own version of the religious issue and tell Him your feelings about living on the basis of the spiritual truth which He has given.

Chapter Eleven

The Applications

It is important that we now stand back and consider some of the implications and applications of all this information about personality types and the spiritual life. Our natural tendency in dealing with such material is to locate our own profile and contrast it with those different from our own, spending most of our time considering only the *personal* applications. Of course this is understandable, and not without benefit. However, even more can be gleaned by viewing the whole, considering how these insights can be used in our ministries to groups and individuals, as well as to ourselves.

Ministry to Groups

✠ *Communication needs for different personality types.* Gordon Lawrence's book *People Types and Tiger Stripes: A Practical Guide to Learning Styles*[1] has been very helpful to me as I have thought about teaching situations where different personalities are mixed together. The following chart contains lessons which I learned from Lawrence, as well as some discoveries which I have made from my own experience as a teacher and retreat leader. As you study this summary, think about how you might apply some of these ideas in your own ministry to groups.

At the outset, it is important for us to recognize our tendency to structure groups and select methods which are best suited to our *own* personalities. However, I believe that it is important for us to consider the variety of people in the group with which we are working, and to reflect on the options available for enabling different types of people to come to grips with the subject matter in a personally meaningful manner. Your exploration of these options will be enriched as you talk to those who are representative of various type groups, finding out directly from them what *they* find most helpful. Continue to incorporate these new findings into your own ministry.

Under each heading I have listed trigger words or phrases which are suggestive of what the various personality attitudes and functions may find helpful in a group setting.

PERSONALITY TYPE AND GROUP MINISTRY

Extroverts	Introverts
Interaction	Reflection
Action	Quiet time
Thinking out loud	Collecting thoughts first
Group projects	Working alone

Sensing	Intuition
Sequential steps	Global view
Visual aids	Reading and listening
Experiential approaches	Lectures
Practical applications	Theoretical perspective

Thinking	Feeling
Gathering facts	Working in harmony
Mastering skills	Expressing empathy
Learning principles	Being person-centered
Achieving intellectually	Giving help
Analyzing issues	Being needed

Judging	Perception
Having things organized	Being unstructured
Establishing milestones	Expressing choice
Being accountable	Having freedom
Maintaining traditions	Remaining flexible
Experiencing closure	Keeping options open

✠ *Some teaching strategies.* In the seminary class I teach on Spiritual Formation, I make use of the following methods and materials in order to relate to the variety of persons present. I have used the appropriate letter (either E/I, S/N, T/F, J/P) to indicate the personality type factor which each teaching method addresses.

> small group discussions (E)
>
> large group discussions (E)
>
> keeping a personal journal (I)
>
> assigned written reflections (I)
>
> lectures (I and T)
>
> using a structured devotional format for daily prayer and meditation (S)
>
> creative projects using some artistic medium (S and N)
>
> videos and transparencies (S)
>
> allowing students to set their own personal goals (S and J)
>
> periodic progress reviews (S and J)
>
> assigning creative writing exercises for journal writing (N)
>
> displaying paintings and playing recorded music (S and N)
>
> assigning challenging books for study (T)
>
> requiring research papers (T)
>
> having students make reports (T)
>
> student participation in small spiritual formation groups (F)
>
> having individual conferences with students (F)
>
> giving personalized feedback and evaluation on student papers in the form of a personal letter to the student (F and T)
>
> using a clear course outline and syllabus (J)
>
> having a "closure experience" to conclude the semester (J)
>
> allowing students freedom in choosing from various options for certain course assignments (P)
>
> using a variety of teaching methods (P)

Four Small-Group Models for Spiritual Formation

I have observed that persons of similar personality types are often drawn to the same kinds of small group experiences for the purposes of spiritual formation. Likewise, group leaders often feel more comfortable leading a particular type of group. The following examples illustrate some of the options. Undoubtedly you will think of many more.

✠ *The Covenant-Discipleship Model provides a structure especially appreciated by Sensing types.* The goal of this model is to strengthen member's practice of devotional disciplines by means of group accountability and support. Participants study some of the means of grace which God has given to us — prayer, Bible study, fasting, the Lord's Supper, and Christian fellowship. They write a covenant together which each group member signs, specifying the minimum commitment of members to the disciplines which have been selected by the group.

At each meeting individuals share their previous week's experiences related to these spiritual methods, and encourage and pray for one another. The predictable agenda of the group meetings, the specific goals, the concrete product (the group covenant), and the regular evaluations of progress are all the kinds of ingredients which are often especially attractive to Sensing persons.

✠ *The Small-Group Bible Study may have special attractiveness to Thinking persons.* The goal of this small group is to study Scripture, a book at the time, "precept upon precept, line upon line." The group deals with background, content, and application, seeking to distill scriptural principles for Christian living. It makes use of lectures, discussions, note-taking, and individual reports. It offers members the opportunity to acquire information, master Bible study skills, and increase competency in the Scriptures. Such goals and processes as these may be especially appealing to Thinking types.

✠ *The Prayer and Sharing Group often attracts Feeling types.* This small group format builds relationships between group members and gives focused attention to the relationship between each member and the Lord. Time is spent getting to know one another, building friendships, and strengthening group trust. This kind of fellowship yields increasing transparency as members share burdens and joys, and pray together for one another. When persons hear others speak their own names and refer to their situations in prayer to God, they know that they've been personally listened to, and that their burdens are being shared by those in the fellowship. They not only sense group support, but they find divine strength and help, for God answers prayer! People tend to follow up with one another between meetings with visits, phone calls, or notes. Such an intercessory group, with these expressions of empathy, support, and mutual helpfulness, taps the special gifts and graces of Feeling types.

✠ *The Great Christian Books Group may be especially appealing to Intuitive persons.* In this group the members take several weeks to read a Christian classic which they've selected, and meet regularly to discuss and share assigned portions. In their reading they contemplate the passages, allowing them to penetrate their very being. They try to read in such a way that the material brings them into contact with their own deepest selves and with God. When they meet together, the emphasis of their sharing is not so much on analysis of the text as it is on its point of contact with their experience, and on the insight and wisdom they're discovering for living a Christian life. As they share ideas and inspirations, they often experience a kind of group momentum, in that perceptions which are shared often stimulate inspired thoughts in others so that there is an intensifying effect for each member. This kind of opportunity to deal with theory and imagery, to rekindle faith and renew vision, touches the special needs of Intuitive persons.

Obviously none of the models listed above are the exclusive territories of particular personality groups. However, you will probably discover, as I have, that they often do have specific appeals—for members as well as for leaders. They serve to illustrate the importance of providing a variety of spiritual growth groups, rather than expecting one mode to apply to all.

A Retreat Model Based on Principles of Personality Type

Retreats provide opportunities for persons to be away from the pressures of their daily routines in order to be together with God. While our usual tendency is to fill retreats with teaching or preaching sessions, we discover that people appreciate opportunities for silence, prayer, and meditation, as well as planned hours when they meet individually with a leader or together in small groups to talk about their spiritual journeys.

We can assist retreatants in their time alone by guiding them to the Word, and suggesting some ways by which they might enter into it and allow it to enter into their own lives. The following suggestions make use of insights from personality type theory.

Format for a Guided Retreat Session

1. Start each session with group worship comprised of Scriptures, prayers, and hymns.

2. The leader tells the Bible story which will be used for individual reflection. In the telling of the story, it is placed in its context and related to the theme of the session and to our everyday lives.

3. Participants receive a list of suggestions for personal reflection on the Scripture, and are allowed to choose the approach which suits them best. A time and place is appointed for people to meet together later with others who chose the same exercise.

4. Individuals are given sufficient time to go away to some quiet place where they can be alone in silence, praying and meditating on the Word, following the particular exercise which they have selected.

5. Small groups gather at the appointed time, and individuals share from their explorations of Scripture, discuss these, and pray for one another.

6. The whole group of retreatants reconvenes and the session is brought to a close in some manner appropriate to the study of Scripture, and to the sharing which has taken place.

Sample Retreat Exercises for Jeremiah 29:1-14

After telling the story behind this passage, the leader would distribute a sheet of paper with the following options for meditation. Retreatants are asked to read the Scripture and then to use the exercise which most appeals to them.

1. What is your own exile situation or experience? Try to imagine that the words of Jeremiah's letter have been addressed personally to you. Rewrite the verses in such a way that they are a personal communication from the Lord to you in your present situation. What meaning do you discover for your situation? What effect is this perspective having on you? What is God saying to you in the words, "I know the plans I have for you"? How is this true for you now? Write a letter to God, expressing your feelings and responses to what He has said to you.

2. Picture yourself as one of the exiles in Babylon. Try to see your situation in detail. What feelings do you have? Visualize yourself at a small gathering with fellow exiles who are listening to this letter being read. How do you react as you hear it? How would you want to respond? When God says, "I know the plans I have for you," try to imagine what that might mean in the immediate future of your own life today ... this weekend. What can you do to respond *concretely* to this word?

3. What is meant when God says, "I know the plans I have for you"? What are your reasons to justify being hopeful? What is the value of hope in your life? How might you practice hopefulness? What are some good examples from Scripture, history, and your own experience of persons who lived with an attitude of hope? What resolutions can you make in order to practice hope and to nurture this quality in your own life?

4. Read the Scripture passage and then go for a walk alone. Choose as scenic an area as you can find. Try to imagine that Jesus is walking right beside you. Ask yourself, "What might I say to Jesus and what might He say to me?" Let your exchange be free and spontaneous.

You might find that the book by Chester Michael and Marie Norrisey, *Prayer and Temperament: Different Prayer Forms for Different Personality Types*, is a helpful resource for developing such exercises as these for retreat or small group settings.[2]

Ministry to Individuals

Spiritual Friendship or Spiritual Direction has been an enduring ministry in the Christian church.[3] It refers to the assistance one person gives to another who has come seeking help in a growing relationship with God. This ministry to individuals is not the sole prerogative of pastors. Some of the most gifted Spiritual Friends in the Christian tradition have been laypersons who are able to serve as wise prayer counselors and spiritual guides. The essential gifts of a Spiritual Friend include:

a vital experience of the Lord

a reflective approach to their own spiritual journey

a commitment to the life of prayer

an understanding of the dynamics of the spiritual life.

You may have found yourself in situations where someone was seeking assistance from you about spiritual life issues. Your helpfulness depended on your capacity to perceive what God seemed to be doing in the other's life, your ability to help the other look at his or her responses to God in the midst of the concrete situations of life, your capacity to listen to the human spirit, and your openness to the Holy Spirit. Another ingredient may also be helpful. Since the other person always meets us through his or her personality, it helps if we also understand the other person's personality type and how it may affect their relationship with God and the church. Such an appreciation of differing creation gifts, potential infirmities, and special ways of nurture and needs for growth often proves invaluable. It may aid us in praying with understanding, listening with awareness, asking relevant questions, and offering appropriate suggestions about the cultivation of the life of prayer. The following chart summarizes ideas from the previous chapters with regard to spirituality and personality type. You may wish to return to the explanations given in the preceding material, in order to fill in the meanings of the various words and phrases in the chart on pages 154–155.

How can we make use of these ideas in our ministry to individuals? I've discovered that people are very interested in understanding themselves better and in seeing how the Lord might help them understand this "self," strengthen and transform it, and use it in His service. In chapter 2, I alluded to a statement by Thomas Merton which I would like to quote in its entirety now.

> Temperament does not predestine one man to sanctity and another to reprobation. All temperaments can serve as the material for ruin or for salvation. We must learn to see that our temperament is a gift of God, a talent with which we must trade until He comes. It does not matter how poor or how difficult a temperament we may be endowed with. If we make good use of what we have, if we make it serve our good desires, we can do better than another who merely serves his temperament instead of making it serve him.[4]

Most persons find great relief and encouragement in such a perspective as that!

There may be times in your work as a spiritual friend to another person when you suggest that he or she read some appropriate section of this book and write a summary of the things they feel are most important. It is crucial to spend time with the other person, talking over these matters, in order to see if he or she feels that the things which have been read in this book actually fit. The other person may say, "That really described me well!" or, "No, that's not really where I am, not how I see myself." This will give them the opportunity to clarify whatever it is that they have been puzzling over. Such increasing self-understanding, as we discussed back in chapter 1, is often essential in the process of spiritual growth.

In spiritual direction, persons we are directing find it very affirming when we point out their gifts and tell how we have experienced them. They often express appreciation for the discovery that their weaknesses are common to those who have such gifts as theirs. They may be thankful to hear that there are ways of prayer and devotion more personally suited to them than those with which they've struggled to be faithful.

HOW PERSONALITY TYPE INFLUENCES SPIRITUAL LIFE

	Gifts	Infirmities	Nurture	Growth Needs
ENERGIZERS ESTP ESFP	action altruism adaptability acceptance artistry appreciation	allurement seduction brinkmanship bravado expediency opportunism	physical spirituality service praying our experiences	reflection faithfulness
STABILIZERS ISTJ ISFJ	thoroughness persistence practicality prudence methodicalness dependability common sense	self-absorption hiddenness suspicion prudishness idolatry perfectionism	quietness structured prayer spiritual continuity	self-assurance playfulness receptivity spontaneity
CRUSADERS ENFP ENTP	ingenuity optimism inspiration creativity originality insight perceptivity	lack of focus independence inconsistency unfaithfulness	vow stability listening prayer image/symbol	Christ-dependence reflection sacrament of present moment
RENEWERS INFJ INTJ	insight vision inspiration motivation possibility	loneliness restlessness indulgence overextended-ness	imaging prayer symbol creative writing	trust intuition sharing insights awareness self-discipline balanced life

	Gifts	Weaknesses	Prayer	Growth
ORGANIZERS ESTJ ENTJ	leadership structure goal-direction decisiveness objectivity formula	tunnel vision impersonality	action mental prayer written prayer rule of life	practice listening seek feedback reflection flexibility surrender of gifts
ANALYZERS ISTP INTP	understanding reasoning commitment to justice reservedness	insensitivity laziness moodiness	mental prayer breath prayer meditation	feeling giving leadership empathy

ENCOURAGERS
ESFJ
ENFJ
	warmth
	hospitality
	loyalty
	idealism
	practicality
	responsibility
		hypersensitivity
		unreflectiveness
		avoidance of
		   unpleasantness
			community
			compassion
			affective prayer
			personalizing
			worship space
				realism
				kindness to self
				openness to
				   critique

ENHANCERS
ISFP
INFP
	mission
	purpose
	warmth
	quiet reserve
	positivity
	hopefulness
	independence
	flexibility
	openness
		feelings of
		   inadequacy
		resistance to
		   reason
		reluctance
		   to share
		perfectionism
			personalizing
			Scripture
			spiritual journal
			listening prayer
				Christ-
				   consciousness
				receptivity to
				   grace
				cultivate
				relationships

They may feel challenged by realizing the areas in which growth might be especially needed, and intrigued to think of how some present situation may be an opportunity for transcending personal boundaries, developing needed qualities with the assistance of God's grace, and depending upon the body of Christ.

The great temptation for any of us when we are learning a new theory or method is to apply it woodenly and without sensitivity. This has happened with personality type theory as well.

It is important to incorporate these insights into our ministry to others, but always with a sense of tentativeness and a kind of playfulness, always open to the other person, recognizing their special uniqueness which can never be boxed up and filed away on some shelf of our mind.

The Lord Who Guides

Man plans his journey by his own wit, but it is the Lord who guides his steps.   Proverbs 16:9, NEB

Become quiet before the Lord. Read Proverbs 15:31–16:16 in a prayerful whisper. As you wait before God, become aware of the specific task or goal which He brings to your mind for decision or action. What plans need to be made? What details might be overlooked?

Prayerfully imagine yourself following through with the plans. Picture various scenarios and in each become aware of the Lord's presence and help. Are any negative memories awakened? Do any apprehensions surface? Allow God to minister to your feelings.

Ask God for clarity and objectivity. Develop steps logically, prepare contingency plans, list persons who need to be involved or who could be consulted.

How deeply do you care about the results? Is your self-image at stake? To whose glory is this dedicated? How will other people be affected by the outcome? Pray for them and for yourself. "Commit to the Lord all that you do."

Chapter Twelve

The Soul's Celebration

We began this book with the question: "Does God ever change a person's personality?" It is not uncommon for our everyday experiences to leave us wondering, "Can God really change me?" Sometimes we struggle with issues raised by our personalities and ask how some of our traits relate to the expression of our spirituality, and how some of our weaknesses are affecting our discipleship.

In previous chapters we have noted some of the ways by which persons with different personality types reach out to the Lord. We have realized that each personality type may display its own special relational dynamics in communion with God. It is important to notice these dynamics and to work with them if there are to be changes in the habits of the heart and in patterns of relating to others and ourselves.

Loving God

There are four insights from our study of personality types which are very important for understanding the process by which our relationship with the Lord is deepened.

✠ *Choosing your path.* While God can communicate directly to our spirits, He usually seems to work through our minds in order to speak to us. On the initial stages of your spiritual journey you have probably noticed, as I have, that we seem particularly attracted to sources of nurture and devotional practices which primarily make use of our favorite mental function (Sensing, Intuition, Thinking, or Feeling). This is simply because we have developed more familiarity, confidence, and skill in that area. Throughout this book you have found suggestions about methods which various personality types may find most natural for nurturing their faith and deepening their consciousness of the Father.

However, in chapter 2, we also observed that during the second half of life, our less-used functions in general and the polar opposite of our creation gift in particular seem to be loaded with possibilities for spiritual renewal and discovery. That is why you may have been attracted to some of the other exercises which were suggested in earlier chapters. By drawing on less-used functions at the appropriate stages of our lives, as the Spirit directs us, we may discover that deeper aspects of our being are becoming more accessible to the Lord. In fact, as we make use of these less familiar ways of expressing our love to God, we may be learning more literally the implications of loving the Lord with *all* our heart, soul, mind and strength—rather than loving Him through only one or two preferred dimensions of ourselves!

You might use the chart on page 161 so that this idea of your "polar opposite" might become more vivid for you. We will return to this chart from time to time in this chapter.

✠ *How to read this chart.* In order for you to appreciate the idea of complementary mental functions and personality types, I have arranged this chart so that opposites are directly across from one another. Let's look, for example, at the Sensing types. If you happen to be a member of this group, comprised of Energizers and Stabilizers, the strength which is complementary to your own is Intuition. It is especially visible in Crusaders and Renewers. Let's take our example down to its next level. If you happen to be a Stabilizer, you may find that Crusaders are the ones whose gifts are especially balancing to your own. Finally, and most precisely, if you are an ISTJ, you might find that your greatest needs for wholeness are the very qualities most native to your polar opposite—the ENFP. So, in this case, the ISTJ Stabilizer who is in the second half of life

**Complementarity Among
Personality Types**

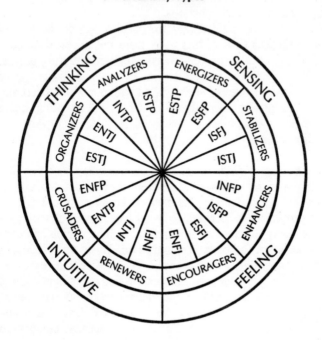

may find some attraction and renewal by utilizing some of the suggestions for faith/nurture which are given to the Crusaders in chapter 5.

✠ *Recognizing your need for balance.* Such growth as we have just described is important not only for the revitalization of our own faith and for the accessing of deeper dimensions of our souls, but is essential for bringing balance to our devotion. By now it should be obvious that we all have an enormous capacity for one-sidedness in our spirituality. Think of the contrast between Extroverts and Introverts. Notice, for example, how Energizers are typically activistic, naturally turned toward putting faith into deeds. On the other hand, Enhancers show a special affinity for solitude and the inner life. Each needs the qualities which the other may have developed. Incarnational service needs to be fed by the bread of inner communion with the Lord; and the inner life needs to find expression in outer actions. Similar observations could be made in comparing each of the sets of mental functions.

You may have noticed that the meditations at the end of each of the chapters of this book have taken you through a fourfold approach to prayer—sensing prayer, intuiting prayer, thinking prayer, and feeling prayer. By praying this prayer of four dimensions, we are seeking God with our whole heart and demonstrating our desire that He have our full attention. It is a simple acknowledgment of our need for balance in devotion and can become a path for growth.

✠ *Opening to fresh experiences.* A deepening love for God also requires our openness to different expressions and experiences of the spiritual life. We have observed some of the variety represented in Scripture. David's demonstration of faith was certainly different from Matthew's. John's approach contrasts starkly with Solomon's, and so on. These manifestations are not simply differences between Testaments, but represent variations of personalities—each expressing an authentic life of friendship with God, but in such surprisingly different ways.

The problem is that all too often we have difficulty affirming this reality in our own lives. For example, because one person is highly sensing and has an underdeveloped intuitive capacity, she may find that when her intuitions are active, they are not only untrustworthy, but are also troublesome. Therefore, she tends to avoid her intuitions, mistakenly assuming that *any* intuitive approach to spirituality is suspect. She may paint the picture even more darkly and say that intuitive approaches are wrong or evil! Such attitudes do three things—they break the bonds of our unity in Christ, they reject others' gifts (which we need), and they attempt to repress aspects of our own lives which are actually crying out for transforming engagement with the Lord.

Take another look at your counterpart on the complementarity chart. Read the description of the spirituality of that type in the appropriate chapter of this book. Then become aware of how you might, even unconsciously, show a critical attitude or lack of appreciation for the spirituality of such a one as this.

✠ *Realizing your dependence on Christ's body.* We really do need each other in the body of Christ. Our experience of the Lord is always partial and it is inevitably impoverished when we keep ourselves from the contributions which others could bring to us. Whatever differences of perception we may have, whatever difficulties in communication, whatever disagreements over courses of action which should be taken, we still need to share together in worship, fellowship, and service with those of different personality types. In this way our understanding and experience of God can be expanded. The communion which grows from such deliberate acts of commitment to one another is a witness to the whole world that Christ has come indeed! (John 17:21)

Loving Yourself

Jesus spoke of the importance of self-love. There are at least four implications from our study of personality type which relate to growing in such a healthy self-regard. Let's summarize these.

✠ *Recognizing your gifts.* Perhaps you have spent far too much of your life wishing that you could be like someone else. You may have been impressed by those who are more energetic and outgoing, or by those who are quiet and reflective. You may have coveted the capacities of those who are practical and down-to-earth, or those who are inventive and imaginative. You may have longed for more skill with critical analysis or empathetic understanding. But now you are coming to recognize your own creation gifts and are seeing that God's birthday gifts for you are good, and they are important for ministry to others. You are increasingly realizing that your differences from others are not deficiencies, but represent distinctive capacities with which you have been entrusted. These qualities of personality are meant to be dedicated to God, cultivated and invested in service to others. Such a view of your life is not narcissism or self-idolatry; rather, it represents the genuine kind of self-love which Jesus urged.

✠ *Understanding your needs.* All too often we find ourselves so caught up in the swirl of life and ministry that we fail to take proper care of ourselves. It becomes a sure path toward burnout. The term *burnout* has practically become a cliché, and in many quarters it seems to have almost become a status symbol for those who claim having had such an experience! However, real burnout can be devastating to the personality and often has tragic results.

We cannot continue to neglect our personal needs for relationships, rest, and recreation without paying a great price in our personalities. If we persist in living stretched out to the limit and beyond, we not only lose our effectiveness, but there is actually a destructiveness and violence done to ourselves and often to those around us. By way of example, Jesus showed us that it is good to care for our needs. Type theory has provided important information about some dimensions of needs requiring our attention if we are to become more whole persons.

✠ *Anticipating your weaknesses.* In each chapter we have looked at the infirmities which we carry within us and which are part and parcel of our humanity. We know these vulnerabilities, sometimes all too well! Real self-love not only involves a recognition of our gifts and a respect for our needs; it also requires a realistic appraisal of our weaknesses. Some people end up shipwrecked on the rocks of their infirmities. Whenever they are not actually falling prey to them, they seem to be engaging in personal sabotage by condemning themselves for even having such weaknesses. However, Paul showed us another way. He has helped us realize that we can actually "glory" in our infirmities, rather than hate them. We can view our vulnerabilities as fresh opportunities for discovering the grace of the Lord, rather than occasions for rehashing the litany of our inadequacies.

✠ *Transcending your boundaries.* Loving yourself also means that you do not sell yourself short. Positive self-regard includes a recognition of your latent potential and unrealized possibilities. It means that when you are faced with demands which seem beyond your finite capacities, you will never underestimate the resources of Christ within, nor the resources of His body around you.

"I am self-sufficient in Christ's sufficiency" (Philippians

4:13, AMP) is a statement made by a man who, apart from Christ, would have never dreamed of taking on the challenges, facing the opposition, or courageously enduring the hardships and sufferings which he received as a result of his commitment to Christ. The resources with which he met these obstacles went beyond what we could call personality type. In fact, we are struck by the clarity of his spiritual insight, the nobility of his concern for others, and the gentleness he showed to his captors through the long period when he was under house arrest and right up to the moment of his death. What we are observing here is the very dynamic of which he said, "My present life is not that of the old 'I,' but the living Christ within me" (Galatians 2:20, PH). His personality had not been commandeered by Christ, but had been surrendered to Him. As a result, he faced life strengthened by this divine friendship and indwelt by this holy love. What we see in the Apostle Paul, and have seen so many times in people of faith, is that *we can be more in Christ than we could have ever been in and of ourselves.*

Personality type is not a box which circumscribes the boundaries of being and the limits of capacities. In fact, God seems to delight in putting us into situations which we would perhaps never have chosen, but in which we can be victorious, simply because we have to rise above ourselves by opening ourselves to His transcendent power.

Loving Others

Finally, Jesus has reminded us that a healthy spirituality requires the expansion of our capacity for loving others. This love, often expressed in the New Testament by the Greek word *agape,* is not sentimentality, but is a personal commitment to seek the highest good for other persons. It implies that we will work and pray that they will find fulfillment, achieve their potential, and become the best they can be in Christ. What are the insights from personality type which can help us grow in such love?

✠ *Appreciating others' gifts.* We can learn to view others from a gift-perspective. This means that we will determine not to concentrate on those characteristics in them which we dislike, but upon the qualities which they contribute. We will try to see how their differences from us can actually fill gaps in our own experiences and abilities. Since none of us are perfectly rounded persons, we will try to keep in mind those areas where we especially need the gifts which others can bring. We will appreciate how they may help us to see things to which we would have otherwise been blind, contribute strength where we would have been weak, be bold where we might have been conservative, or be cautious where we might have been foolhardy. Paul's image of the body, with each organ and appendage working together in harmony, is a powerful one. While he was writing about our mutual ministry through our spiritual gifts, I believe that his image is further amplified when we add our understanding of creation gifts.

Return to the complementarity chart once again. Think of the persons with whom you seem to have the greatest difficulty relating. Often, though not always, these are persons who have personality types which are across the chart or at least in a different quadrant from your own. Use this insight to guide you in considering their gifts, praying for them in their needs, and praising God for their ministries.

✠ *Responding to others' needs.* Loving implies that we will try to be aware and understanding of others' needs as well as their gifts. We will try to grow in our respect for personality differences, not demanding that others become like us, nor even that they must always adapt themselves to meet our own peculiarities! Rather, we will seek to know them well enough to understand what they need from us, and then try to meet them more than halfway. For example, in communication we will try to speak to the Sensing person's need for concreteness and detail, or the Intuitive's need to see the big picture and the guiding vision. Likewise, in decision-making, we will respect those whose Feeling orientation causes them to evaluate matters from the standpoint of personal values, or those whose Thinking orientation causes them to focus mainly on objective considerations. In group life, we will honor the more reticent members who tend to think things out before speaking, and we will try to create ways for making sure we receive their input, rather than allowing those who are more verbal to dominate the time. Paul reminds us that we are to think more highly of one another than we do of ourselves (Philippians 2:3). We might paraphrase his comment by saying that we are to so highly regard and respect the perspective and contributions of others that we are more concerned to receive from them than we are to defend our own viewpoint or have our own way. Who knows what would happen if everyone in the group showed such a spirit of love!

✠ *Dealing with conflict.* Conflict is inevitable. Since we do have differing perspectives, and since we often take very different things into account in our decision-making, we are bound to experience misunderstandings and differences of opinion. Christian unity does not mean the absence of conflict, but requires our willingness to lay aside defensiveness, the urge to protect our turf, and our anxious concern to assert our rights. In Ephesians, before Paul began speaking of our gifts, he spoke of the necessary graces.

> I urge you then—I who am a prisoner because I serve the Lord; live a life that measures up to the standard God set when He called you. Be humble, gentle, and patient always. Show your love by being helpful to one another. Do your best to preserve the unity which the Spirit gives by the peace that binds you together.
>
> Ephesians 4:1-3, GNB

Such attitudes enable us to be receptive to one another and to the Lord. A quiet and receptive spirit and the willingness to wait upon God in prayer are essential if we would discern the will of God together. Although there is such variety of personalities among us, nevertheless, there is "one Lord, one faith, one baptism ... one God and Father of all, who is *above all, and through all, and in you all*" (Ephesians 4:5-6, italics added).

✠ *Allowing for others' growth.* Love gives to others the same respect which it desires for itself. We would never want another to judge our abilities to perform in the future simply on the basis of what we did in the past. Each of us is on a journey. Each is in the process of growth. Understanding others' personality types is a way of honoring people because it shows our desire to understand what is important to them. However, our appreciation of their uniquenesses should never be used to circumscribe our estimates of their capacities. Rather, we will seek to recognize growth and celebrate God's ways working in both of us.

> God has chosen what the world calls foolish to shame the wise; He has chosen what the world calls weak to shame the strong. He has chosen things of little strength and small repute, yes and even things which have no real existence, to explode the pretensions of the things that are—that no man may boast in the presence of God.
>
> **1** Corinthians 1:27-29, PH

What Sort of Person Are You?

Think what sort of people you are, whom God has called.
1 Corinthians 1:26, NEB

———————————————————————

Using at least two different Bible translations, read through 1 Corinthians 1:26-31 twice in a whisper. Listen to the words. Underline portions which are especially striking. Copy one special verse onto a plain card, using your best penmanship.

Imagine yourself alone with Christ. Allow Him to speak the words of your special verse to you. Let the full implications begin to soak in.

List the contrasting words or phrases which Paul uses to make his point. Think of examples of the worldly wise who've proved foolish; of seemingly weak and insignificant persons through whom God has worked powerfully. How was their weakness turned to strength? What was the effect?

Pour out your feelings to God in a prayer of gratitude, repentance, and rededication.

Personality Type:
A Basic Reading List

The Myers-Briggs Personality Type Theory

The following books will guide you to a deeper understanding of personality type theory. *Gifts Differing* and *Please Understand Me* also have rich descriptions of the sixteen personality types.

Keirsey, David, and Marilyn Bates. *Please Understand Me: Character and Temperament Types*. Del Mar, California: Prometheus Nemesis, 1978.

Lawrence, Gordon. *People Types and Tiger Stripes: A Practical Guide to Learning Styles*. Gainesville, Florida: Center for Applications of Psychological Type, 1979.

Myers, Isabel Briggs. *Gifts Differing*. Palo Alto, California: Consulting Psychologists Press, Inc., 1980.

_____. *Introduction to Type*. Gainesville, Florida: Center for Applications of Psychological Type, 1976.

Myers, Isabel Briggs, and Mary H. McCaulley. *Manual: A Guide to the Development and Use of the Myers-Briggs Type Indicator.* Palo Alto, California: Consulting Psychologists Press, Inc., 1985.

Schemel, George, and James Borbely. *Facing Your Type.* Wernersville, Pennsylvania: Typofile Press, 1982.

Spirituality and Personality

These books will be helpful if you are interested in other attempts to relate our understanding of personality type to Christian spirituality.

Bryant, Christopher. *Prayer and Different Types of People.* Gainesville, Florida: Center for Applications of Psychological Type, 1980.

Clark, Thomas E. "Jungian Types and Forms of Prayer," *Review for Religious.* September–October 1983.

Grant, W. Harold, Magdala Thompson, and Thomas Clarke. *From Image to Likeness: A Jungian Path in the Gospel Journey.* New York: Paulist Press, 1983.

Harbaugh, Gary L. *Faith-Hardy Christian.* Columbus, Ohio: Augsburg Publishing House, 1986.

_____. *God's Gifted People.* Minneapolis: Augsburg Publishing House.

Keating, Charles J. *Who We Are Is How We Pray: Matching Personality and Spirituality.* Mystic, Connecticut: Twenty-Third Publications, 1987.

Michael, Chester P., and Marie C. Norrisey. *Prayer and Temperament: Different Personality Types.* Charlottesville, Virginia: The Open Door, Inc., 1984.

Oswald, Roy M. and Otto Kroeger. *Personality Type and Religious Leadership.* The Albin Institute, Inc., 1990.

Further Reading
in Spiritual Formation

The following materials are suggested to help you increase your understanding of Spiritual Formation and, more importantly, to help you grow in your faith. Readings are categorized under basic headings having to do with our formation. Most of the books are in print at the time of this compilation. The few which are not can be obtained from most college and seminary libraries in your area. In addition to these resources, please use the footnotes as a further means of exploring the various topics developed in this book.

General Readings

1. Leslie Weatherhead, *The Transforming Friendship*
2. Steve Harper, *Embrace the Spirit*
3. Maxie Dunnam, *Alive in Christ*
4. E. Stanley Jones, *The Way*
5. Henri Nouwen, *Making All Things New*
6. Evelyn Underhill, *The Spiritual Life*
7. Alan Jones & Rachel Hosmer, *Living in the Spirit*

8. Iris Cully, *Education for Spiritual Growth*
9. Benedict Groeschel, *Spiritual Passages*
10. M. Robert Mulholland, *Invitation to a Journey*
11. Ben Campbell Johnson, *To Will the Will of God*

History of Christian Spirituality

1. Urban Holmes, *A History of Christian Spirituality*
2. Alan Jones & Rachel Hosmer, *Living in the Spirit* (helpful chapter)
3. Gordon, S. Wakefield, *Westminster Dictionary of Christian Spirituality*
4. James M. Gordon, *Evangelical Spirituality*
5. Jones, Wainwright, & Yarnold, *The Study of Spirituality*

Devotional Classics

1. Tilden Edwards, *The Living Testament: The Essential Writings Since the New Testament*
2. Thomas Kepler, *An Anthology of Devotional Literature*
3. *The Upper Room Devotional Classics*
4. Paulist Press Series, *The Classics of Western Spirituality*
5. Jim Smith and Richard Foster, *Devotional Classics*

Prayer

1. Harry E. Fosdick, *The Meaning of Prayer*
2. Dick Eastman, *The Hour That Changes the World*
3. Kenneth Leech, *True Prayer*
4. Anthony Bloom, *Beginning to Pray*
5. Maxie Dunnam, *The Workbook of Living Prayer*
6. Albert Day, *An Autobiography of Prayer*
7. William Paulsell, *Rules for Prayer*
8. Richard Foster, *Prayer: The Heart's True Home*
9. O. Hallesby, *Prayer*
10. Jean-Nicholas Grou, *How to Pray*
11. Lance Webb, *The Art of Personal Prayer*

Scripture

1. Robert Mulholland, *Shaped by the Word*
2. David Thompson, *Bible Study That Works*

3. Susan Muto, *A Guide to Spiritual Reading*
4. Thomas Merton, *Opening the Bible*
5. H.A. Nielsen, *The Bible as If for the First Time*
6. Thelma Hall, *Too Deep for Words*
7. Carl Olsen, *Find Yourself in the Bible*

Direction/Accountability

1. David Watson, *Accountable Discipleship*
2. Tilden Edwards, *Spiritual Friend*
3. Kenneth Leech, *Soul Friend*
4. Thomas Merton, *Spiritual Direction*
5. Edward Sellner, *Mentoring*
6. William Barry & William Connolly, *The Practice of Spiritual Direction*
7. Carolyn Gratton, *The Art of Spiritual Guidance*
8. Robert Coleman, *The Master Plan of Evangelism*
9. Jim Smith, *The Renovare Workbook*

Discipline and Disciplines

1. Richard Foster, *Celebration of Discipline*
2. Dallas Willard, *The Spirit of the Disciplines*
3. Gordon MacDonald, *Ordering Your Private World*
4. Albert Day, *Discipline and Discovery*
5. James Earl Massey, *Spiritual Disciplines*
6. Maxie Dunnam, *The Workbook of Spiritual Disciplines*

Family Spirituality

1. Marjorie J. Thompson, *Family, the Forming Center*
2. Brian C. Taylor, *Spirituality for Everyday Living*
3. Ernest Boyer, *A Way in the World: Family Life as Spiritual Discipline*

Fasting

1. Richard Foster, *Celebration of Discipline* (helpful chapter)
2. Tilden Edwards, *Living Simply through the Day* (helpful chapter)

3. Arthur Wallis, *God's Chosen Fast*
4. David R. Smith, *Fasting: A Neglected Discipline*

Ministry and Spiritual Formation

1. Edward Bratcher, *The Walk-on Water Syndrome*
2. Henri Nouwen, *The Living Reminder*
3. Louis McBirney, *Every Pastor Needs a Pastor*
4. Henri Nouwen, *Creative Ministry*
5. Oswald Sanders, *Spiritual Leadership*
6. Eugene Peterson, *Working the Angles*
7. Alan Jones, *Sacrifice and Delight*

Personality Type and Spiritual Development

1. Harold Grant, *From Image to Likeness*
2. Christopher Bryant, *The River Within*
3. Chester Michael, *Prayer and Temperament*
4. Gary Harbaugh, *God's Gifted People*

Social Spirituality

1. John Carmody, *Holistic Spirituality*
2. William Stringfellow, *The Politics of Spirituality*
3. Dietrich Bonhoeffer, *Life Together*
4. Thomas Kelly, *A Testament of Devotion* (helpful chapter)
5. Henri Nouwen, *Gracias!*
6. Henri Nouwen, *Compassion*

The Holy Spirit/The Gifts of the Spirit

1. Billy Graham, *The Holy Spirit*
2. Kenneth Kinghorn, *The Gifts of the Spirit*
3. Donald Hohensee & Allen Odell, *Your Spiritual Gifts*
4. Myron Augsburger, *Quench Not the Spirit*

The Lord's Supper

1. William Willimon, *Sunday Dinner*
2. William Barclay, *The Lord's Supper*
3. Martin Marty, *The Lord's Supper*

Devotional Guides and Prayer Books

1. Reuben Job, *The Upper Room Guide to Prayer for Ministers and Other Servants*
2. Bob and Michael Benson, *Disciplines for the Inner Life*
3. John Baille, *A Diary of Private Prayer*
4. Charles Swindoll, *Growing Strong in the Seasons of Life*
5. John Doberstein, *The Minister's Prayer Book*
6. *The Book of Common Prayer*

Determining Your Favorite Function

The idea that you have a favorite or dominant mental function is very important in the Myers-Briggs approach to personality type theory. The four mental functions are sensing, intuition, thinking, and feeling. One of these four will be your favorite. Because of your preference you will depend on this process, and will probably feel more comfortable when you are using it than when you are operating out of one of the others. Your favorite function is a central characteristic in your personality.

Two of the mental functions, Sensing and Intuition, have to do with how you *perceive* things. These are called the Perceptive functions. The other two mental functions, Thinking and Feeling, relate to your way of coming to *decisions*. These are called the Judging functions.

Introverts use their favorite function in a different manner than do Extroverts. The *Introvertive* person prefers to use the favorite function to deal with *inner* things. This private world of thoughts, ideas, and reflections is their energy source. On the other hand, the *Extrovertive* person uses the favorite function to handle *external* matters. Their attention gravitates most naturally toward the outer world of people, situations, and external stimulation, where they draw energy.

You might think of the difference in the use of the favorite mental function in terms of contrasting management styles. The Extrovert's dominant function is the kind of manager who is always accessible, directing operations on the floor. The Introvert's favorite function is like the manager who is back in the office, checking the systems, planning new products, making critical decisions behind the scenes. It is usually easier to get to know Extroverts. Their strength is used to meet people and to deal with the world around them. It takes a little longer to get to know Introverts. Their strength is kept behind the scenes in order to handle the priorites of their lives.

The flow charts which follow will guide you in discerning your dominant function. Take your type letters ("ENTJ" or "INFP") and using the appropriate chart, circle each of your letters. This should make each step in the explanation more meaningful for you.

First, let's look at the Introvertive person's favorite function. The numbers on the left-hand side in the following chart correspond to the four steps in the explanation below it.

INTROVERT'S FLOW CHART

HOW TO FIND YOUR DOMINANT FUNCTION

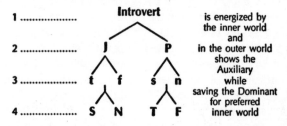

1. The chart on page 180 is used only for the Introvertive persons (those whose first type letter is "I").

2. The last letter of your type ("J" or "P") refers to pre-ferred lifestyle. If it is Judging, follow the "J" path to the next level. If you have a Perceptive lifestyle, follow the "P" side.

3. The Introvert shows the outer world the auxiliary or helping function. Introverts who are "J" will show their Judging functions (either "T" or "F") in the outer world. Introverts who are "P" will use their Perceptive function ("S" or "N") to the outer world.

4. The Introvert's dominant or favorite mental function is saved for their highly valued, internal work. If you are "J" in the outer world, your favorite function will be a Perceptive one (either "S" or "N"). If you are "P" in the outer world, your favorite function will be a Judging one (either "T" or "F").

EXTROVERT'S FLOW CHART

HOW TO FIND YOUR DOMINANT FUNCTION

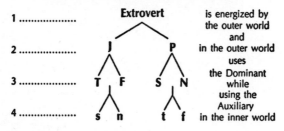

1. Use this chart when searching for an Extrovert's domi-nant function (those whose first type letter is "E").

2. The last letter of your type ("J" or "P") relates to your lifestyle in the outer world. If it is Judging, follow the "J" path to the next level. If your lifestyle is Perceptive, follow the "P" path.

3. By definition the Extrovert uses the dominant or favorite

function in the outer world. Step 3 indicates your dominant function from among your type letters.

4. The Extrovert uses the auxiliary or helping function to deal with inner world matters. If your dominant is a Judging function (either "T" or "F"), your auxiliary will be a perceptive one (either "S" or "N"). If your dominant is a Perceptive function ("S" or "N"), your auxiliary will be a Judging one ("T" or "F").

Notes

Chapter One

1. C.S. Lewis, *Mere Christianity* (New York: The Macmillan Company, 1960), 175.

2. Isabel Briggs Myers, *Gifts Differing* (Palo Alto, California: Consulting Psychologists Press, 1980), 1–10.

3. *Theologica Germanica of Martin Luther*, translated by Bengt Hoffman (New York: Paulist Press, 1980), 69.

Chapter Two

1. Thomas Merton, *Thoughts in Solitude* (New York: Farrar, Straus and Giroux, 1983), 22.

2. Isabel Briggs Myers, *Gifts Differing* (Palo Alto, California: Consulting Psychologists Press, 1980), 14–16.

Chapter Three

1. Helpful descriptions of this group are found in David

Keirsey and Marilyn Bates, *Please Understand Me* (Del Mar, California: Prometheus Nemesis, 1978), 196–99.

2. Isabel Briggs Myers, *Introduction to Type* (Palo Alto, California: Consulting Psychologists Press, 1987), 18.

3. _____. *Gifts Differing* (Palo Alto, California: Consulting Psychologists Press, 1980), 103.

Chapter Four

1. Eusebius, *Ecclesiastical History*, vol. I, translated by Hugh J. Lawlor and John E. Oulton (London: SPCK, 1954), 101.

2. Isabel Briggs Myers, *Gifts Differing* (Palo Alto, California: Consulting Psychologists Press, 1980), 104–8.

3. Ibid., 108

4. Ibid.

5. I first saw this observation in a one-page leaflet prepared by Earle C. Page, "Following Your Spiritual Path" (Gainesville, Florida: Center for the Application of Psychological Type).

6. Ibid.

7. "A Conflict of Visions: Ideological Origins of Political Struggles," *Time*, March 16, 1987.

8. Isabel Briggs Myers, *Gifts Differing* (Palo Alto, California: Consulting Psychologists Press, 1980), 105.

Chapter Five

1. Isabel Briggs Myers, *Gifts Differing* (Palo Alto, California: Consulting Psychologists Press, 1980), 109.

2. Ibid., 109–10.

3. Ibid., 57.

4. Ibid., 110.

5. Hannah Whithall Smith, *God Is Enough*, edited by Melvin E. Dieter and Hallie A. Dieter (Grand Rapids: Francis Asbury Press, 1986), 255.

6. Jean-Pierre De Caussade, *The Joy of Full Surrender*, translated by Hal M. Helms (Orleans, Massachusetts: Paraclete Press, 1986), 14.

Chapter Six

1. William Temple, *Readings in St. John's Gospel* (London: Macmillan & Co. Ltd., 1963), xxv.

2. Isabel Briggs Myers and Mary H. McCaulley, *Manual: A Guide to the Development and Use of the Myers-Briggs Type Indicator* (Palo Alto, California: Consulting Psychologists Press, 1985), 45.

3. Thomas à Kempis, *The Imitation of Christ,* paraphrased by Don Demaray (Grand Rapids: Baker Book House, 1982), 43.

4. Julian of Norwich, *Showings,* translated by James Walsh (New York: Paulist Press, 1978), 130, 183.

Chapter Seven

1. Isabel Briggs Myers, *Gifts Differing* (Palo Alto, California: Consulting Psychologists Press, 1980), 85–87.

2. Ibid., 86.

Chapter Eight

1. Isabel Briggs Myers, *Gifts Differing* (Palo Alto, California: Consulting Psychologists Press, 1980), 89.

2. See for example Gary Smalley and John Trent, *The Language of Love* (Waco, Texas: Word Books, 1988).

3. Isabel Briggs Myers, *Gifts Differing* (Palo Alto, California: Consulting Psychologists Press, 1980), 91.

4. Ron Delbene, *The Breath of Life: A Simple Way to Pray* (Minneapolis, Minnesota: Winston Press, 1981).

Chapter Nine

1. Excellent descriptions of this group are found in David Keirsey and Marilyn Bates, *Please Understand Me* (Del Mar, California: Prometheus Nemesis, 1978), 167–70 and 192–94. See also Isabel Briggs Myers, *Gifts Differing* (Palo Alto, California: Consulting Psychologists Press, 1980), 93–97.

2. Christopher Bryant, *Prayer and Different Types of People* (Gainesville, Florida: Center for Applications of Psychological Type, 1980), 9.

Chapter Ten

1. J.D. Douglass, Organizing Editor, *The New Bible Dictionary* (Grand Rapids: Wm. B. Eerdmans Publishing Co., 1962), 755.

2. Isabel Briggs Myers, *Gifts Differing* (Palo Alto, California: Consulting Psychologists Press, 1980), 98.

3. Ibid.

4. Ibid., 97

5. Ibid.

6. Dietrich Bonhoeffer, *Life Together*, translated by John W. Doberstein (New York: Harper and Row Publishers, 1954), 26–39.

Chapter Eleven

1. Gordon Lawrence, *People Types and Tiger Stripes: A Practical Guide to Learning Styles* (Gainesville, Florida: Center for Applications of Psychological Type, 1982), 49–55.

2. Chester P. Michael and Marie C. Norrisey, *Prayer and Temperament: Different Prayer Forms for Different Personality Types* (Charlottesville, Virginia: The Open Door, Inc., 1984).

3. I have found a helpful introduction to this special ministry to be the book by Tilden Edwards, *Spiritual Friend: Reclaiming the Gift of Spiritual Direction* (New York: Paulist Press, 1980). This source contains an excellent bibliography which will carry you more deeply into the subject.

4. Thomas Merton, *Thoughts in Solitude* (New York: Farrar, Straus and Giroux, 1983), 22.